SHIPPED OFF

GORDON BLITZ

DEDICATION

to my husband Neal, sister Elyse and her family.

He hates being confined to this wheelchair. Who cares if he said the view was exceptional? Yes, if he wasn't crippled. The Santa Monica horizon stares back at him. The blonde surfers in their black wet suits seek a wave to welcome their morning. Where are the life coaches? life guards? Each deep breath digs into the chest. Hammering pain is nailing the man to the chair. Heart attack? Anxiety? This deserted space is safely away from the homeless. June's cruel gloom days find an outlet in his vulnerable depressive state. Perched above Pacific Coast Highway on Ocean Avenue, the view of the pier does nothing to enlighten the mood. The frigid extremities are slowly defrosting as the sun gathers strength. Looking for a distraction to avoid wallowing? Tunneling through a landmine. Careful not to step on explosive recalls. The death memory is not comforting. Dead parents, dead careers, and dead nerves. The numbness reaches from his hip to his little toe. Wanting to prove he still has some physical ability before bed sores snack on his body, is a fantasy goal. But dragging the leg is exhausting. Cry a little more. The colonic tears are not doing their job.

****

Sunday January 3, 2016 10:00 a.m. Santa Monica

GORDON

My shoes felt like bricks. When I took my ten thousand-step walk around Santa Monica, each bone in my foot crushed against the cement sidewalk. I forged on, ignoring the pain. The doctor told me it was tendonitis. Since walking was my only tolerable exercise, I couldn't follow his directions to ease off. Mentally I was unprepared to give up my only source of raging endorphins. Walking was breath to me especially since my daily anti-depressant Wellbutrin hadn't been working.

I recognized Matt from a block away by the outskirts of the Santa Monica College campus. The bounce in his step was his calling card. His five-ten muscle-laden frame was irresistible. His unruly silver hair gave him a goofy joy. We hug.

Friends for twenty years and he doesn't realize I've had a crush on him. I'm petrified to jeopardize this rock of a friendship. My ten-year age difference is a severe stumbling block. His addiction to younger men makes me off limits. And I'm not a gym junkie like Matt. I'm not 'his type' is an unspoken language of our friendship. But Matt's shallow traits are overshadowed by his genuine charitable kindness. He volunteers as a big brother. He gravitates towards the homeless. Matt will share food and money with street people.

Matt is a legal secretary for William Morris Agency. The attorney he works for, handles contracts for television writers and producers. He puts in gargantuan hours but at least he's well paid.

"Matt, I want to throw something out to you. I have this phobia about water. My therapist insists I take a cruise to alleviate my fears. Would you consider taking one of those cheapie Mexican Riviera seven-day Carnival Cruises?"

"I don't know. I've never been on a cruise. Will I get seasick? Stir crazy?"

"No, they tell me it's mild waters. I've heard there is so much to do. They have a workout room, pool, entertainment, piano bar, and all the food you can eat. It's $600 for seven days."

"Really. Let me think about it."

"It's the one-year anniversary of my mom's death. This funk I'm feeling is frustrating. I feel like I've been cooped up in my condo. The solo walking, I do is lonely. The cruise would force me to confront passengers."

"Okay it's only seven days. I haven't had a vacation in years. And maybe it will do my skin some good. I never get enough sun. And the sea air will help my allergies and asthma. Sure, I'll go."

I love his spontaneity. I booked the cruise within a day. We would depart from Long Beach the first week in March. Two months to get ready. Matt convinces his boss to give him the time off with a promise that when he returns, he'll work on a contract for some big honcho Television producer. They're doing a reboot of a classic sit-com from the nineties. Matt acquires sea sickness patches for both of us as a backup. Our first cruise.

Thursday March 3, 2016 1:00 p.m. Long Beach

GORDON

The grueling check in process takes hours in Long Beach. Our ship is called Carnival Splendor. This floating city towers over us as we wind our way up the gangplank. The shaking of the gangplank as we walk aboard nibbles away at my confidence. I have seven days to fight off my neurotic ocean fears. Then a photographer stops us. And when I put my arm around Matt's shoulder, I'm disappointed that Matt doesn't stare into my eyes for the snapping picture.

When we finally get to our cabin we collapse from exhaustion. We squirm through the tight efficiently used cabin space. The furnishings are miniaturized. And the bathroom is like a compact cage for only one animal. The small porthole is very different from the brochure explanation of ocean view. The twin beds are separated. Standard practice setup unless the cabin steward is notified. I wish they'd been accidentally aligned.

As long as I don't look at the ocean, my phobia seems to be in check. The gentle movement reassures me that I can handle this. I cleared the hurdle of the safety drill where rescue operations procedures were detailed if we hit an iceberg. My therapist would be proud.

After dinner and the ship's Broadway-themed entertainment, Matt suggests we check out the bar where Friends of Dorothy are meeting. This is a sweet homage to Judy Garland and the *Wizard of Oz* appeal to gay and lesbians. The glass elevator sweeps us to the upper stratosphere of the ship. We stroll to the Cruiser Bar. We don't recognize anyone remotely gay or lesbian. We order a couple of beers and nurse them as we wait for our people to arrive.

"This is a bust. Maybe we are the only gays on this cruise." I explain.

"Come on let's go to the disco. Maybe we'll see guys there."

"It's on the next level. Follow me."

Sure enough, when we hear the blasting decibel music there are a bunch of guys dancing together. We join in. You can't go wrong with Janet Jackson. "Runaway" from her *Design of The Decade* is filling the room. The deejay has the pulse of the crowd. Twenty years ago, that was on the charts. God 1995 was a good year.

I was thirty-five. Dreariness hadn't clutched at me. My lover Harry and my mom were alive. I just want to dance. An unfamiliar song pumps the floor and disgusts me as my energy begins to lag. The ringing in my ears is annoying.

Matt escapes and gravitates toward some young twinkie.

"Matt, I'm going back to my room. I've had enough." I scream into his ear. *How can you spend time with this infant?* I wanted to say. Matt is such a contradiction. He's vice-president of our temple. He tells me how much time he spends in committee meetings. Trying to increase membership. He has such a strong belief in God and yet he's acting like a jerk tonight.

He smiles as I leave. My anger is in check on my walk back to our deck and cabin. I could kill him. I just assumed he'd follow my lead. Tonight, would have been a night I could pounce but I'll be in slumber land when he drags himself back. Maybe he'll be respectfully quiet and I won't notice. I am exhausted. Nothing is going to interrupt my sleep.

The beds are richly inviting with the top sheet delicately pulled back. A bird shaped by a white towel sits on my bed. Chocolate candies circle the bird. A card says *My name is Alfonso. I'll take care of all your needs during your seven-day cruise.* I love being taking care of. Sleep comes easily and lasts for eight hours.

****

Friday March 4, 2016 morning-stateroom
GORDON

When I feel the grinding of the engines under the room, I realize we must have reached our first port, Cabo San Lucas. Matt's bed is unruffled. He must have gotten lucky last night. No wonder I wasn't disturbed. We don't have an excursion but we can leave the ship within an hour of docking. I didn't bring my cell phone so I don't have an easy way of finding Matt. We don't have assigned tables for breakfast. He must have gone to the buffet. Or he's sleeping in with his conquest. I'm starving. I want some nourishment.

The buffet is mobbed. The cafeteria setting must appeal to the masses. The crowds want to take advantage of the 8:00 a.m. to 5:00 p.m. scheduled time in this port. Beach and drinking are the only reason to visit Cabo San Lucas. I'd be happy to just sit on the ship and read my kindle. *My Ex-Life* by Stephen Mc Cauley is mindless gay literature. After I grab my scrambled eggs, turkey bacon, lox, roasted potatoes, and gluten-free pancakes, I search the dining room for Matt. The harsh lighting over a sea of overweight humans should make Matt easy to find. To keep the crowds moving, servers attempt to clear piles of left overs off the Formica tables. My patience leaves the building. He's not in my sightlines. Oh well, I'll just eat alone. At least I should get a table that has a view of the city. The startling view of the port makes me want to rethink my negative opinion of Cabo. When I go back to the cabin, I'm sure Matt will be there or left a note.

As I use my key card to enter, I am bombarded with silence. Matt's bed remains unwrinkled. No message in a bottle. I look at the phone and see a blinking red light. Must be a message from Matt. I quickly maneuver the buttons to get to the voice mail. What I hear is "Welcome aboard. As a new guest we are offering you a free bottle of champagne during any of your meals. Just come by guest relations to pick up your voucher."

Damn. Why haven't I heard from Matt? What is going on? I need to figure out if Matt has left the ship. There must be a log to track visitors to Cabo. How else are they going to know if they've left anyone behind when we depart later today?

I look for the Cruise Director by the pool deck. He's in the middle of Sexiest Man on Board contest. It looks like he's picked a bunch of overweight millennials. I'm told to go to the bowels of the vessel where the office for missing persons exists. Is that really a place? How can you disappear on a ship?

When I enter the office, I refrain from any niceties and tell the officer, "I'm looking for my friend, Matt Schulman. The last time I saw him was at the disco last night. He was wearing a very loud Hawaiian shirt." The nautical photos on the wall don't comfort me.

The uniformed man tried to look concerned as I explained the situation. His comb over hair weakens my confidence in his expertise.

"Maybe he's disembarked?" he asked.

"That's why I'm here. Do you have a passenger manifest so you can check that out?"

"It's ten o'clock now. We docked at eight so it's possible. Give me a second while I contact the departure deck. I can ask them to check. I'm pulling up your friend's information now. We have a picture on his Passport I.D. That will help."

He shows me the picture. Not a great photo of Matt. The picture is five-years old. He had brown hair with specks of grey. And his skin was clear. No sign of pimples and blackheads. I am starting to feel weighted down. My gut is pulling apart. The tight room without windows is making me nauseous.

"Can I get something to drink? I don't feel well."

"I'll get you some water."

Thankfully I am sitting or I might have passed out. This is not how I expected to spend the first morning of the cruise. Damn you, Matt. Where the hell are you? Why do I feel like I'm always the caretaker? I was responsible for Harry when he was diagnosed with AIDS. The burden of my mother becoming a widow at thirty-six started my history of co-dependency. I thought Matt could take care of himself. I'm tired of being a caretaker.

"Okay, we'll go through the list and figure out where he is. You need to go back to your room. Relax. We'll find him. My name is Henry Stillman. If you hear anything contact me ASAP."

"Does the Captain know what is going on?" I ask Henry.

With a blank non-responsive answer, he opens the door and escorts me into the hall. When I hear his bland afterthought, "Don't worry." I curse, "Fuck" to myself.

I'm in a fog as I walk back to deck five. The ice sculpture demo at 11:00 a.m. has lost its appeal. As I enter our cabin, I notice the steward has returned the room to its original manufactured condition. Squarely made beds. No signs of occupants. We had unpacked each of our seven-day cruise outfits in the tiny closet. The space nakedness is horrifying. The porthole is a poor excuse for light. I need *My Ex-Life* Kindle to smother me. As I begin reading, I find I am possessed with images of Matt kidnapped or falling off the ship and drowning. Too bad I am so proficient in projecting negative thoughts. The ringing phone startles me. Henry begins talking, "Yes, yes. I understand you're upset. Apparently, Matt never left the ship. We have no record of him disembarking."

"What do you mean? So, he's somewhere on the ship?"

"It seems that's the case. We have cases of guests getting lost. This is a large ship. There are over two thousand passengers."

"So, can't you find him. Do we need a search party with torch lights?"

Without a hint of a lone laugh he says, "We're trying. Was he depressed at all?"

"No, what are you talking about?"

"We're just trying to rule out things. "

"Rule out what? Oh my god. You think he jumped overboard. That he committed suicide. No, that is impossible."

"We're just checking. It's happened before. You never know what is going on in someone's head."

"Matt would never try to kill himself. Just find him." I can't breathe. This cannot be happening.

"What about the kid he was dancing with at the disco. We need to find him."

"What kid? You mean a child?"

"Everyone looked like teenagers. The disco was so dimly lit and with the foggy strobe lights I couldn't tell much about who he was dancing with."

The benefits of the sea air are battling the Cabo San Lucas humidity. If I continue this robotic persona maybe I can get through the afternoon. I need distraction. Do I become my own search party? Stalking the corridors hunting for Matt. No if he's really lost it would be an obscure space on the ship. The engine room? I wouldn't have access. What about the bunker area where the crew sleep?

I wish I was a more devout Jew like Matt. Then I could pray to God. But I am such a realist. It would be hopeless praying. I did see that there would be Shabbat Services tonight. I hope that community feeling might alleviate my descent.

My love hate relationship with religion began after my Bar Mitzvah. My father died a month after I became a man. The four years of Hebrew school left me unprepared for being fatherless. God had abandoned me. Friendless in Long Island. Mom was grieving and I couldn't console her. She stayed in bed with the duvet coverlet wrapped around her body. When I nudged her to make me breakfast, she ignored me. Our Cape Cod became a prison fortress. No siblings. And mom was an only child too. Then my father's family shut us out. Orthodox grandpa had told Mom, "You know in the Jewish religion, a widow should marry one of her husband's brothers." Mom refused.

I turned to an imaginary friend, Mr. Watercan. I would talk to him about God.

"Why did God let my father die? He was only thirty-nine. He kept complaining about a pain in his chest. The stupid doctors didn't do anything until it was too late. And I don't want to go back to school. The kids hate me. They make fun of me and they hate Jews. And those horrible things they say about blacks. Those spitballs hurt. I want to kill myself. Wouldn't I be happier if I was dead? What should I do, Mr. Watercan?"

Silence.

When we moved to Los Angeles in 1973, my world altered. Gone were the brittle Long Island winters. Living six blocks from Fairfax Avenue cinched membership in the Jewish tribe. But the bullying was back in full force, and then I met Carl.

His flaming red hair caught my eye. He had a cute pudginess about him. I heard girls giggle as we walked out of English class at Fairfax High. In the hall I ran up to him. His unique brand of feminism gave him a startling appearance. He gave off a womanly vibe that bordered on caricature. Months later, when I met his mother, I felt like I was watching a carbon copy of her mannerisms.

"Hi. Isn't Mrs. Blaine a great teacher? I love that she is making us read *The Confessions of Nat Turner* by William Styron."

"She seems like a hippie. I'm Carl."

"Hi, my name is Gordon."

I had no real friends and I was relieved Carl didn't dismiss me. Two loners looking for a common thread. Finally, an easy person to talk to. I had been a transplant from Long Island for two years. We talked about music. "Don't you love the Carpenters? I didn't have to worry about sports or how I walked or talked. Our friendship cemented. We spent our time running to movies, eating out and listening to music.

A month later I nervously looked at Carl and spit out, "Carl, I love you. I haven't felt this way about anyone before." We tried kissing. I didn't know where to put my tongue. I had never felt the deep inside of someone's mouth before. I was shocked he didn't pull away. We didn't speak. I didn't feel anything sexual. Disillusion grabbed hold of me.

The frightening aspects of my friendship with Carl were compartmentalized. My only acquaintance was Peter. He had a nerdy quality that made him invisible. We spent most of our time bicycling. After he met Carl, he told me, "Why are you friends with him? He is so weird. He's like a little girl." I didn't respond. I was used to being made fun of. How was Carl any different? My sixteen-year-old brain didn't quite get it.

Then things really soured. What happened next has remained vivid as though it was happening in real time.

At my apartment I hear a knock. Carl is standing there," I've got the new single by the Carpenters: *Solitaire*."

We scurry into my bedroom. Slipping the 45 out of the jacket and gently putting the needle in the groove we wait a second for the intro. Karen's warmth emanates from the speakers. We hear a banging noise.

"Hey, someone must be at the front door. I wasn't expecting anybody." I look through the peep hole and see it is Peter. Oh, my goodness.

"Hold on Peter," I holler through the door. The music is still blasting from the bedroom. I run back to Carl.

"You've got to hide. Shut the music off. Peter can't see you here."

Carl looks perplexed, "Why what's wrong?"

"Just get in the closet until I get rid of him." Carl obeys me. I go back and open the door.

"Hey Peter. What's going on?"

He tells me, "I was in the neighborhood and wanted to stop and say hello."

He barges in. My heart is fluttering as I worry that Peter will discover Carl.

"Peter, I have homework to do. I'll call you later."

Peter leaves and I go back to the closet where Carl is still hiding.

Carl looks confused as I pull him out. I don't let him speak.

"Come on let's listen to The Carpenters."

"What happened? Why were you hiding me?" Carl asked. I couldn't answer him. I started the record and turned up the volume.

A month slips by and a chubby girl comes towards me. Despite her acne and bulging weight, I found her appealing. She has a sparkling smile, "Hi, my name is Loren." I am shocked that a girl would talk to me at Fairfax High School. My reputation of being a sissy hovered over me. Loren says, "Have you thought about becoming Christian? If you believe in Jesus, he would save you from your sins."

I told her, "But I am Jewish."

She said, "It doesn't matter. Jesus was a Jew."

I remember my neighbors in Long Island telling me that Jews had murdered Jesus. I didn't know what they were talking about. I wasn't religious. With the death of my father after my bar mitzvah, who needs God?

Loren asked, "Why don't you come with me to the Presbyterian church in Hollywood. They have a youth group and a born-again Christian guitarist."

I envisioned that dating girls would make my life simpler. I wouldn't be ostracized if I had a girlfriend. There wouldn't be a Carl that I needed to hide. I wanted to try Christianity. I needed the persecution to end. Loren had told me I should accept Jesus as the savior and receive the holy spirit.

When we go to the church Loren introduces me to the female pastor. "Hi, Gordon. Loren told me all about you. Follow me into my private office." It felt so strange to be in a room filled with crosses and pictures of Jesus on the walls. She asks if I want to become Christian and I say yes. I close my eyes and wait. Nothing else. Just ask and receive. She puts her hands on my shoulder. "Do you accept the holy spirit? Is Jesus your savior?" I repeat yes, many times. I am confused because I don't feel any different. I was inpatient. I had fantasized that my tormented isolation about my sexuality would disappear. It was buried but still eating at me.

I ask the pastor, "Is there anything I need to do?" She smiles and congratulates me.

As I descend the stairs, I see Loren with a grin on her face. "I guess I am Christian now." I see a tear in her eye. She gives me a hug. We make plans to see a film the following week.

Two weeks later I receive a letter with Loren's return address.

Dear Gordon,

You need to break off your friendship with Carl. He is a devil and will destroy your life. He is a feminine homosexual man that will corrupt you. I cannot continue to associate with you until you dissolve your connection to Carl. The Bible says homosexuality is a sin. You can never truly be saved.

I begin to sweat as I read her words. What? My best friend would ruin me? The only person I had professed love to should be banished. How did Loren even know about Carl? She must have seen me talking to him. I followed her directive and called Carl.

"Carl we can't be friends anymore" There is a pause. "Loren says I can't have you as a friend."

"Who is Loren?"

"I met her in history class. She thinks you are gay and corrupting me," I explained.

I feel the devastation emanating from Carl. I start quivering. I can't keep talking to Carl. I ripped him from my world. I felt cleansed.

Later I call Loren, "I am no longer friends with Carl. I want to go out with you on a date."

After a long pause she says, "I am so relieved that Carl is out of your life. Gordon, I have been so worried about you being degraded by Carl. But honestly, I am not interested in you romantically."

I feel a punch in my gut. I hated how I let religion twist me. I couldn't look into my eyes. This was my initiation to what shame felt like. It took two years before I had the courage to ask Carl to forgive me.

Twenty-three years later religion popped into me when I joined the oldest gay and lesbian temple in the world, Beth Chayim Chadishim. Matt is a member of the GLBT temple I belong to which makes our friendship rigorously permanent.

Matt was my go-to person when my drama queen was out of control. After my lover Harry died and I went on my quest to find a husband he kept track of each boyfriend. Matt never got tired of hearing me say, "This is the one." When my accounting position abruptly ended, he pumped me up with a clear plan. Why not retire at fifty-five? He convinced me I was flush. He refused to let me wallow in depression. He was my emotional caretaker. And when my mom died, Matt insisted I sleep at his apartment till my wrecked emotions subsided. Matt was the kind of good friend who let me sob without offering useless clichés to embolden me.

Twenty years of daily conversation. He knows my secret horrors. I'm never afraid to reveal any of the monstrous actions I think I've made. When I placed Harry in a hospice rather than taking care of him, Matt never judged me. Mom lived alone and it was catastrophic for me to visit her daily. Organize caregivers. I would find her on the floor. Incapacitated. It broke me. As an only child, it fell to me. And when I decided to have mom move into my condo, I was told I was insane. That parenting my mom would slay me. After five years of intimately caring for her, I put my mom in a nursing home against her will.

Matt adored my mother. He was parentless due to early deaths of his mother and father. He let me make my decision. Other friends and relatives told me, "It will kill her if you do this." I didn't have an option. Her dementia had worsened. The caregivers couldn't prevent falls. If I left mom unattended for a few hours when her caregivers vacated the premises, I found stove burners left on and running water from faucets. Mom attempted to swallow her hearing aids. She died within six months of her nursing home residency.

He spoke sparingly. His love propped me up. More than a lover. No strings. No complications. Matt was the one. If only I could be brave and profess my closeted romantic love for him.

The solitude after mom died made room for severe seclusion. The condo haunted each room she had saturated. The same space that Harry had populated. The crippling plague dragged me to hell. But at least there was Matt.

These sweet memories of Matt propel me into a nap. Two hours pass before my neck screams stiff from my awkward sleeping position. A shower and shave could refresh my faith that Matt will be found. I turn up the hot water so that it burns my follicles. Scratching away dead skin with my nails feels orgasmic. Shedding my negative thoughts. It's way too early for our late dinner seating. I can lose myself in the piano bar. Croaking through *The Piano Man* or *Those Were the Days* will be a distraction.

I feel a jolt and growl. The floor is barking at me. Oh no. We're leaving Cabo San Lucas. It's 5:00 p.m. already. The captain is announcing our departure. Are they 100% sure Matt never departed? Did they factor in the human error for those passengers who disembarked without the normal channels? Shit, where is Henry's number? I want him to assure me that we haven't left Matt behind. I am making myself crazy as the ship leaves port.

I leave the cabin and find my way to the closest view of Cabo. I bravely look at the city without glancing at the water motion. Another jolt and a quiet breeze hits me. Motion stops. The engine dies. I'm comforted by the stillness. Then I hear a scream from the other side of the ship. A piercing animalistic shout. Repeating shouting screams. What is going on? I circle back through the lobby on to the other side. A crowd is gathering. Leaning over the edge. Pointing towards the water. People are hugging the railings.

"Man overboard. Help!"

My God. Is it Matt? Did someone float to the surface just as we were disembarking?

I push passengers away and try to grasp an image. The uniformed officer begins scattering the crowd and stops me. He tells us, "Please step away from the edge. We are trying to figure out what is in the water. Please go back to your cabins. We'll be making an announcement once we pull the object out of the water."

That's what they are calling a body, an object. This can't be happening. I ignore my nausea as I view the open ocean.

"Sir, my friend has been missing since last night. Could he have fallen overboard?"

"We don't know. As soon as we fish it out of the ocean we'll know more."

As the crowd disperses, I remain cemented to the deck. I'm not leaving. I want to watch the rescue mission. I find a corner to hide. The empty deck quiets. I edge towards the railing. As I peer towards the ocean, I see two men struggle to lift something. It's small. Why is it so difficult to snatch? Oh no it doesn't look like an adult. Could it be a child? How horrific. Wait a minute. It looks like a life size doll. Is this a joke? I am walking through a nightmare.

I hear the officer complainingly laugh, "How could someone be so stupid to throw a doll into the water?" I want to scream my revulsion after listening to the explanation.

When I return to my cabin another Henry call pops, "We haven't gotten any traction from the deejay who might have seen him. No one has come forward. This boy you said was dancing with Matt. We can't find him either. The security staff has been searching for Matt without success," Henry explains.

"Wait a minute. Are you telling me someone else is missing?"

"We're not sure." Henry explained.

"How can you not be sure?"

"There hasn't been a missing person report besides Matt. What if this boy was traveling alone and didn't know anyone? Well you can see where I'm going. We wouldn't have been notified. Do you know what it would be like to have two thousand passengers line up and get checked against the sailing list?"

"But that's what you have to do."

Henry continued, "Even if we did that, what would it prove? That the two of them are hiding or stuck someplace on the ship. We've been looking and we can't find anything."

I pleaded, "At least you'd have a picture of this other boy. Someone could identify them."

My anger is in the stratosphere. How can they be so incompetent? I collapse on the cabin bed and try to nap. The swelling tendons in my feet remind me how crippling each step I take, looking for Matt. I ignore the pain. And a combined middle back spasm pain is competing with my feet for attention. I hear some commotion in the hallway and open my door.

I see the steward, Alfonso and ask him to come into the room. "Alfonso, have you ever heard of a passenger missing before?"

"Yes, but don't tell management. I don't want to lose my job. It happened last year. We sleep in bunkbeds in the bottom of the ship. The engine room is nearby and there are these dark passageways. A passenger got stuck behind a gigantic pipe. When they found him, he was dead. He was diabetic and he was in a coma. It took forty-eight hours to discover the man."

****

June 2016 Santa Monica

This pitying sorrow is eating his guts. Watching television and playing with the internet doesn't wipe away boredom. Hoping that at the next doctor's appointment, good news will come out of the doctor's mouth. His mantra of being patient is annoying. The once-a-week physical therapy hasn't made a difference. The body is disappearing. The wasting process is in full force. He appreciates being cared for but mixed thoughts of a hidden agenda scare him. Guilt. He said he would repair him. Does he mean it? And when and if he returns to his version of normal will he still feel that way? He'll be blamed for what happened.

****

Thursday March 3, 2016 11:30 p.m. Top Deck
MATT

I can't believe Gordon went back to his room. It's so early. Not even 11:00 p.m. I hope this was a good idea traveling with him. We are so different. I'm a night person. That's when I'm most productive. And Gordon is so cheap. He never mentions giving to charity. When he sees someone homeless, he walks by them as though they are invisible. I always give them a dollar. I bet he didn't stay at the disco because he would have to buy a drink.

Damn it, Gordon is my best friend. I would have walked on the outside deck with him if he didn't bail. The clear night makes stars visible. I could have pointed out The Big Dipper. Now I'm asking for trouble on this dance floor. All the guys are in their twenties. I'm setting myself up to get hurt.

This guy I'm dancing with never stops moving. I wonder if he's high on something. I don't even know his name and we've been dancing non-stop for an hour. I won't need to go to the gym on the ship after this cardio dance workout. He looks familiar. Maybe temple? I usually only date Jewish guys and that isn't coming through with him.

His model perfect features from his petite ears to straight lined nose make me gasp. The aroma combines an animalistic ferociousness with an aching scent.

He grabs my hand and takes me back to the bar area. His nails are bitten down to their stubs. The cuticles are ragged with some dried blood. Otherwise his hands emanate a sexual warmth and tenderness that electrifies me. His hands never stop moving. The sound decibels are diminished so we can talk without shouting.

"I'm Matt. And you are?"

"Daniel G. Let's get shots. See if you can keep up with me."

I ask the bartender for five shots each.

"What is the G. for?" I ask.

"I just like the way it sounds. My middle name is Gregory which I hate. But I love the way Daniel G. rolls off my tongue. When I got to Cal State Northridge, I added the G and when I become a big star it will easy for people to remember."

'Oh, you're an actor."

"And I'm trying out for American Idol. I'm a double threat."

"Have we met at the William Morris Agency? I work there for Harvey Blendsome. He's the attorney for writers. I'm his legal assistant."

Daniel's eyes begin bulging as he closes into my chest. "If you like, I could introduce you to theatrical agents."

He starts moving his tongue over his lips. What a flirt. I notice his 501 jeans aren't buttoned. Ready for action? And of all times my acne is flaring. I thought that was a teenage dilemma. Whoever heard of adult acne except for my dermatologist? And I'm not going to use makeup to cover the pimples. Daniel's vibrant skin combined with my blemishes will make for fireworks. Daniel holds my face in his hands.

Will this angel be willing to have sex with me? I hate when Gordon or temple members complain about me only dating younger guys. I'm never going to be a father. I like the idea of mentoring a young person. Offering them a history of things I enjoy. Classical music, Opera, ballet. And since becoming a big brother at the YMCA, I am changing the world. These kids are missing a parent and need a father figure.

"Have I seen you in any movies or television shows? Local theater?"

"I want to show you a secret place on the ship. You'll love it."

"Have I seen you at my temple BCC?"

Why is he ignoring my questions? I look at the bar counter and realize all our shots have been swallowed. No wonder I'm feeling heavenly.

He grabs my hands and rips me off the bar stool. His giggle is infectious. What is it about this strange boy? We're walking through the halls at a slow jogging pace. It's almost midnight and the walkways are barren. We're headed toward a dimly lit sign that says *Danger, Don't Enter*. Daniel pushes the door open. I expect an emergency bell to echo through the vessel.

"Come on chill. Don't be afraid."

"What about the sign on the door?"

"I don't follow rules, Matt. I do what I want."

The moment we move through the door a grinding sound clogs up my ears. There is a steep staircase leading us down to what looks like the engine room. As we maneuver our way through the narrow spaces, I start to perspire. The propulsion engines are spewing hot air. And I start coughing from the dirt and dust tracking under our steps. I should have brought my inhaler. I don't want to have an asthma attack. Daniel seems oblivious to any discomfort. His consistency is stronger than mine. Oh yeah, he's twenty years younger. His stride is still at a quick pace. I follow his lead.

"Daniel, what is so special about this? I can hardly breathe."

"Don't you see the beauty of these shiny engines? They are the guts of the ship. It's moving tons of weight through the ocean. It is such a feat. I mean there are almost three thousand passengers including the thousand crew members. Just a little further and you'll see my favorite spot. Listen to the gears humming. It's like a mechanical symphony serenading us." His expressive hands are mesmerizing me as they point to these images.

I can't believe he sees the poetry of the machines. I stop Daniel so I can stare into the soul of his eyes. Our eyes lock. It feels like divine eternity until we break apart.

As I begin following Daniel again, it's becoming so tight that we're rubbing against greasy machinery. My clothes will be stained and filthy. I see a small bench in the corner. This must be what Daniel is talking about. As I move towards the corner I freeze. Why can't I move? Oh fuck. I'm stuck. How was Daniel able to get through? Did he turn sideways? I wasn't paying attention.

"What's wrong, Matt? The magic bench is waiting for you."

"I'm stuck. I can't move. Can you help me?'

"Let me see if I can pull you through. Can you turn to the side?"

"No, I'm afraid I'll hurt myself. I'm getting scared."

Daniel tries pulling. Tugging at my muscles, ligaments and tendons. I feel like I'm being torn apart.

"Daniel, do you have any WD40 you can spray on me so I can slide out of here?"

"Oh good. You still have a sense of humor."

But the pain is getting intense. I'm having trouble breathing. I'm in a vice."

Daniel shoves me, "Ow!" I scream as he squeezes me through. Thank goodness I'm free.

This release reminds me of my trip to Santa Fe with my boyfriend, George. The first time I understood what panic attack meant. Sometimes I wish I was more like Gordon. He's not afraid to admit his mental health issues. I feel like I have this image to uphold. I would never go to therapy to deal with panic attacks. And I never would take anti-depressants that Gordon swears by.

The flat Santa Fe skyline paints our drive from Albuquerque. I feel God's presence. The volcanic red pressed against the dark highway as we stare beyond the naked road. The windblown tumbleweeds give a spooky aura to the scenery. The natural moon light illuminates our trip. Mozart's 41st Jupiter radiates through our car rental. An easy hour commute will take us to George's rental home in Santa Fe. He wants to sell the two-hundred-year old adobe home on Acequia Madre Street. George told me after ten years of being a landlord, the Santa Fe rental market has dried up.

While we are in Santa Fe, Rossini's *La Cenerentola* at the Santa Fe opera will provide an excuse to enrapture us. The partially covered Opera House welcomes the astrological planets and stars to enhance the brain cells gulping the music.

We begin the process of checking into the old-world charm of The St. Francis Hotel. Liz, the hotel manager, had been a permanent fixture for thirty years. She greets us with, "the honeymoon suite." A private twinkle joke for us. The lowest priced room had no view. The concise space peppered with antique furniture symbolized our romance. A compact ritualistic relationship. The centerpiece of the room is a print of Georgia O'Keefe's Jimson Weed that stirred us to physical contact.

Our first meal takes us to Café Pasqual less than a block from the St. Francis. Outside the restaurant, a line of locals and tourists is ensconced from opening to close. The Tex-mex egg dishes abundantly fill each plate warning the patrons that they can easily fast for the next eight hours.

The spiritual lunch awakens a scratchy talk.

"I'm thinking about why we stopped visiting Santa Fe annually," I ask.

"The air fare became outrageous. There were so many other states and countries that I wanted to take off my bucket list."

"We haven't been having any sex, George. It's been months."

"I don't want to talk about it." He's getting back at me about not being monogamous.

His eyes droop with, "I just haven't been in the mood. It takes so much out of me."

This is why I like much younger men. George is my age but talks like an old man.

Even with his frown I am unprepared for, "How am I supposed to get excited? And you never shave on the weekend. Your stubble feels like sandpaper on my face."

"But you won't talk. What do you want to do?"

"I want us to move in together. We've been a couple for five years. Wouldn't it be easier for you to be faithful if we were under the same roof?" he pleads with me.

I can't answer so I nudge toward George remembering that during our drive to Santa Fe, his right hand would periodically leave the steering wheel and crawl towards me. The bristling hairs on my knuckles tingled. The silence vibrated through the Chevy Bolt car rental. Mozart's symphony glided us to a finale.

It's been a month since the last Santa Fe tenant returned their keys and departed. Larry and Bill were superior tenants. The carefree couple cared for the home like it was a prized possession. They cultivated charm. For the last ten years there wasn't a peep out of the lovebirds complaining about plumbing issues, appliances, or rain intrusions.

Larry and Bill honored us with a home-cooked dinner on our last visit. They were closet interior decorators. Each fabric, painting, rug, and fixture was an authentic antique. They could combine the antique delicacies with modern chic Indian pieces. It all worked. The meal was their joint effort. As their lightning limbs worked in unison to create stuffed chicken lathered with sauce, we were struck by their dance. I could hear a melody in the preparation. My cooking was always a solo effort. I knew George would make a simple recipe complicated.

After lunch at Café Pasquale, I ask, "George, before we go to your house can we walk around downtown? I love the farolitos. Those little bags of candles and sand that are lit each night by hand. It's the closest I get to appreciating Christmas. The nippy cold December weather gives me frostbite nightmares. Fifteen degrees is difficult to adjust to. The hush tones of the red bags distract me from the icy temperature."

"Wow. You used to hate coming here. Now it's a spiritual experience. Sure, we can make the detour."

The stretch out of the car stirs my blood. The chill hits my nostrils as I suck in a deep breath. The sky is bombarded with twinkling stars. A canopy protecting us. I wish George would grab my hand.

When we get to George's condo, the meditation stops as George struggles to find the keys. Finally, when we enter the abandoned living room the ghosts of Larry and Bill's warm textured earthy furniture haunts us. The emptiness makes us gasp. In the bathroom I try to wash my hands.

"George, there's no hot water." I shout.

"I wonder if the water heater was shut off," George explains.

I follow him into the kitchen area. He opens up one of the cabinets and begins inspecting the water heater. It looks dead to me.

"Matt, we need a match to relight the heater. Look around in the drawers."

"Found something. Here try these."

George tries the matches but there is no spark.

"These are dried out. Damn. I wonder if any of the neighbors are around to help."

It's part of a four-condo complex. I check another drawer and smile at the long fireplace matches. The unopened box gives me hope they'll work.

The sizzling sound of flame means we are on our way to hot water. A hot shower would be a magical dream to warm my bones. I go back to the bathroom to check the water. As I turn the faucet, I hear a loud noise. An explosion of sound bombards my ears. The rumbling under my feet is earthquake terrifying. What is going on? A propulsive gurgling rumbles against the faucet. In a flash water bursts through the floor. I am standing in rushing water. The flash flood quickly works its way up my shins to my knees and I am in frigid water.

"Help Help," I scream. Can George hear me with all this noise? What is going on? I try to wade through the water to find safety. As I move to the hall the walls around me start to seep water. Is the adobe melting? I start coughing. The water is saturating my pants. The ocean of water is filling up with some sort of plaster seeping out of the walls. Where is George? I'm having trouble breathing. I need to remember to always bring my inhaler. Must have left it at the hotel. I'm scared to take a deep breath. Who knows what is in the soot?

I hear George's faint voice, "Matt, where are you? I'm stuck in the kitchen. The doorway collapsed. I'm trapped."

Oh no. How are we going to get out of this? A few moments of calmness after hearing his sweet voice are starting to dissipate. Another gigantic explosion. Oh God what is that sizzling sound. Is that an electrical spark? My god, did the water expose an electrical wire? Am I going to be electrocuted? I'm way beyond panic mode.

"I'm going to die. What should I do? Help," I scream.

"The pipes must have burst. I need to shut off the water. I've forgotten where the valve is? Damn it," George yells.

"I think I see a live wire. Shit, what am I supposed to do? Do you have your cell phone, George? Can't we call someone?" I cry out. George is so cheap. He should have a management company take care of this place.

"No, I left it in the car. Just stay calm. Don't move and don't touch the wire. Just give me a minute to figure this out."

"I'm starting to feel numb in my feet. I'm in icy water. I can't stop shivering," I shriek.

"I just thought of something. Aren't you near the back door? Can't you escape that way?"

"There's so much cloudy dust I can hardly see anything. And it's hard to move in this water. I can't believe your neighbors haven't heard the racketing blasts." I try to roar back.

I blindly move away from the loose wire into the hallway. I can't remember where the back door is. We haven't been to Santa Fe for many years. Not with the perfect tenants who never complained. There was never a need to visit.

A bright light illuminates the room. The hot water heater has exploded. I start to squint. Is this a mirage or is there a rescue team?

The savior voice hollers, "Hold on. We're trying to pry open the door and get you out."

"Can you shut off the electricity? This wire is sparking. I'm scared." I tearfully cry out.

I hear a combination of voices talking, "We're looking for the water shut off. Better check the fuse box and take care of that. Stay away from the wire and then don't move. We'll get to you soon enough."

I've never had a real panic attack. Now I know what that feels like. If my knees would stop clattering maybe I could breathe for a moment. I can't even feel my feet anymore. The tingling went away and I'm left in a paralyzed state. Come on, rescue team. Hurry up. I don't even hear George anymore. What's happened to him? Is he okay? Shit, I've just been thinking about myself. Damn.

The backdoor opens and George glides in with another man. They put their arms around my shoulder and help me walk. Their touch erases my frostbitten nerves. I drag my feet through the squishy water covering the remains of the wood floor. The outdoor fifteen-degree temperature has chilled the water. I'd like to dunk myself in a hot as hell jacuzzi and spend an hour in a sauna. I never want to feel cold again. When I embrace George, I evacuate this nightmare. I refuse to stop kissing. I'm never going to refrain from the loving tears. The rescue liberation storms through me. I'm released. I wanted this to be a turning point. But George kept pushing for us to cohabitate and when I refused, the relationship dissolved. I went back to dating young guys. And I became more involved with the temple. My belief in God surged. So even if I couldn't have a successful relationship, I would be able to be intimate with God.

Now, I don't know if I can trust Daniel. He's a wild card. "You're crazy. Why did I follow you? I feel like I've been through a juice strainer." I tell Daniel.

"Oh, don't be a baby. Damn You. We're alone with the machinery. Fuck." He bursts off me and gallops towards the stairs.

Is he having a temper tantrum?

When he turns around and bats his eyelashes, "I'm sorry. I thought you would enjoy this."

"I do. It's just what if someone finds us down here."

"It's the middle of the night. No one is looking for us. Here have this. You'll feel better."

"What is this? Are you trying to drug me and have your way with me?" I joke.

"Come on. You'll love the way these poppers work. You'll feel blessed."

I must be nuts to do this. Why do I let myself get into these situations with young guys? I'm setting myself up. Still, I dare myself and sniff the poppers. The effect on my nostrils is startling. What would Gordon think? He doesn't even drink. What would he say about Daniel? When he used to date it's always with potential husbands his own age. But he sabotages relationships by rushing into love. And recently he's become reclusive. I can't imagine being tied to one person. Monogamy would never work for me. And I enjoy living alone, making my own story each day.

"So, where did you get the poppers?"

"I have friends. Trust me. You'll be swept up in an orgasmic high. I swear its pure ecstasy. And the sex will be amazing. You hardly sniffed. Do it again and really inhale."

He's right. The second inhalation is selling my soul to exhilaration.

"Uh oh. You mean we're having sex down here? On this bench?"

"What are you afraid of? It will be so hot." His eyes are bleeding with trust. I've lost all sense of rationale. This is so different from being in the sauna at the Twenty-Four Fitness Gym and having a stranger jack me off. This is provoking an alarm that I'm ignoring.

"Just chill." Daniel begins taking off my shoes. As he peels off my white athletic socks, he caresses each muscle and tendons in my feet. His fingers massage the ball of my foot. Lightning explodes through my legs. He takes his mouth and begins sucking on each toe. All I can think about is nothing.

"I told you I would take care of you."

When he pulls away from my toes, I moan, "Don't stop." Daniel removes my shirt. As it drops to the floor, I notice some blood stains. Must have scraped myself. I let Daniel languish his sensuality on my arms. Free me. Leave me breathless. Take me feverishly inside of him. I relish this spiritual connection with Daniel. As I inhale the poppers again, I move into the stratosphere of an orgasm. Amnesia work your will with my mind. I could be Daniel's teacher. And his egotistical demeanor makes him perfect for the acting profession. I'm intimate with the world of agents. Daniel would be a work-in-progress lover. Time elongates.

****

Friday March 4, 2016 7:00 a.m. Daniel's cabin

MATT

I start drifting. My eyes are shuttering. I can't pry them open. The pressure is swelling my facial muscles. I'm gripped into immobilization.

My mouth is parched sandpaper. Crusts are seeping out of my corneas as I untangle. I can't turn my neck. It's cemented to my right side. I'm disoriented. My watch says 7:00 a.m. Those poppers must have wiped out the last six hours. Where am I?

This must be Daniel's cabin. It's so dark. I feel like I'm in the bowels of the ship with no window. I try to escape the clutches of the bed. I need to pee. The ship is still. I think this is our first port, Cabo San Lucas.

Where is Daniel? I see an image hovering towards me. I mumble, "Are we still in the engine room, Daniel?" The image frightens me. I hear voices. "Where is his wallet? Don't worry this will make him sleep all day." Fingers approach my head. White specks come into focus when I glance at hands. Pills are being popped into my mouth. My lips form the words, "No more poppers." But no sounds escape. They are being forced by my teeth as my head is held back. An explosion of water gets shoved down my throat. The refreshment soothes the anxiety fright for a moment. Then I'm drowning in water. It's gone down the wrong windpipe. I try to cough. I've lost control of my reflexes. My memory of screaming help is vacuumed into space.

February 15, 2016 11:00 a.m. Santa Monica

DANIEL

I enjoy standing in front of the mirror in the apartment and checking out my looks until my roommate Steve knocks on the door and enters with, "I can't do the cruise."

"What do you mean?"

"An emergency came up at work. They won't let me go. I told them about the Carnival Cruise."

"So perf, I'm supposed to go alone. Shit. Damn, it's only seven days. You're only missing five days of work. We've been planning this for months." Steve's eyes keep darting back and forth. It's like he doesn't know how to look at me.

"Sorry not sorry, Daniel. I'm slaying the job at Google. I don't want to take any risks losing it. And I'm up for a promotion in Mountain View at their headquarters. You know how to turn up. It's easy for you to meet people. You're lit. And think about having the cabin all to yourself. You can bring back guys and not worry about me. It's woke. And Google said they'd reimburse me for the cruise so I'm not losing anything."

I'd like to beat him to a pulp.

"That's great for you, Steve." I'm angry now. "I have to bounce for school."

I can't believe Steve would do this. A spineless wimp. So basic. You don't just change vacation plans at the last minute. Steve is getting back at me for not wanting to have sex. I should have known having him for a roommate would be problematic. He's the poster millennial for a couch potato. His distended stomach makes him look way older than his twenty -four years.

When I moved in with him last year I said, "I don't think we should even consider having sex. I don't want to jeopardize the roommate arrangement." I thought he agreed to the terms. He's an immature kid. Steve's pasty skin has never been exposed to sun. His addiction to video games rules his life. He'd be a contented man gaming and streaming twenty-four seven. Why would I want to sleep with him? And he's a druggie too. He brags to me about these uppers he takes so he stays awake until four in the morning. He's addicted to Vicodin also. Marijuana is the furthest I'll go with drugs. And when he masturbates, he uses poppers. He told me all his nerve endings are on fire when he jacks off. I'm going to make an exception and bring the poppers on the cruise; they could be beneficial. Steve won't care if a few of his treasures are missing.

I need to get out of this lame apartment. I shouldn't be nervous so why am I nibbling at my fingernails? Ouch, I'm bleeding now. Where are the Band-Aids? Oh, forget it. I have to get to class at Cal State Northridge. I should be killing it with this theater arts degree. The life coach counselor said you need a Bachelors. It's bullshit. With my face, who needs a degree?

The reality is that I'm twenty-five and I haven't had a decent job. I mean working at California Pizza Kitchen is sick. The tips are okay and they are flexible with my schedule, if I ever get an audition. This cruise was supposed to be a reset button. Figure out what direction I want to go. And plus, I'd get to grind with some hot older guy. I love any form of maturity in a man. Bald, grey hair, the beginning of crows-feet around the eyes. I've seen pictures of Steve Martin when he was forty. His premature grey hair made me erect. But I do have my limits. No old guys over forty-five. I hate trolls. No senior citizens.

My fantasy is to meet some well-established man who can support me. I had a scheme to get a Jewish husband at temple Beth Chayim Chadishim. The guys are wealthy stunners. I love that Jewish swagger.

But it was a bust. I felt invisible after services. Like there was a sign plastered on my forehead saying, "Not Jewish." Oh, a few of the younger congregants spoke to me. Boring millennials. They were reeking of poverty.

I'm swerving until I become a dope superstar. I can humble-brag with these coal black eyes and this Mexican Riviera Cruise is going to be woke. Who cares if I'm alone? Steve would have crimped my style.

Thursday March 3, 2016 11:00 P.M. Top Deck of Ship
DANIEL

This is a pitiful disco. So tacky. The garish decorations are pathetic. What kind of strobe light is twirling on the ceiling? Is this for children? This cruise is so second class. Thank God Steve isn't here. He would have complained from the get-go. And we would have been eating each other's throat in the inside miniscule, windowless cabin. I checked in early and unpacked. Leaving the room fully dressed for dinner means I don't need to go back until I want to sleep. I'm too claustrophobic in the stateroom. Especially being alone. I'm not going to spend any time sitting in my room. Since I left the room at three, I've been surveying the ship. Chatting people up and getting a few rays of sun.

At the very least the first stop in Cabo will give me a winter tan. But now I'm into a horny jurisdiction. A mere pittance of men are within the disco space. Damn. Oh, wait who is this guy with the grey-verging on white hair? I'm thirsty from his angular face. When I checked my Susan Miller astrology, she said a voracious Gemini would be excellent. I need to ask about his birthday. The colors on the shirt are outrageous. But he's shredded. And his ear lobes are luscious. Even with a few hairs sprouting from his ears, this man is choice. And that acne on his chin gives him a bad boy quality. But I can't assume he's gay after what happened earlier.

"Hi there. You must dance with me." I pull him off the bar stool. I nestle up to him then gyrate across the dance floor. I don't care if he thinks I'm an exhibitionist flirt. He's going to be mine. Let's see if he can keep up with me. Those arms have been chugging weights but if he's a sweater I'll wear him down.

After some basic small talk, I realize the sweet coincidence that he works at William Morris. His June twelfth birthdate is wow. I want to make this night ratchet. Take him on an extraordinary journey. When I was studying the cruise details, I typed in secret places on a cruise ship just for fun. Apparently, the engine area is spooky and sexy. Awesome technology guiding the monster ship. Is Matt up for danger? And I have these poppers that will make for an extra sexual experience. It should guarantee one-hundred percent success with Matt. And if I can make him fall in love with me, he'll feel compelled to use his connections at William Morris to get me an agent. I am smelling like a star already. Our contest of drinking shots is an omen.

Since my parents disowned me five years ago, I've been floundering. You'd think being gay wouldn't be the crime of century in 2010 but my small-minded parents were in a bubble. Their religious right doctrine was horrifying.

And they guilted me about all the surgeries they paid for. I am thankful that my scoliosis was corrected. Because I was in and out of body casts between surgeries, I was off school for six months. Then I wore a brace for two years. Between the stares and laughing of students, it's a miracle I got through grade school without a breakdown. Damn, it was worth it unless I was going to play the hunchback of Notre Dame.

We moved from Cleveland to Los Angeles when I started Highschool. A new start. No one knew about my spine curvature. I started having sex with guys when I was sixteen. It was natural. And I was such a good actor, I could pretend I was straight in front of my parents and peers. Being into guys wasn't wrong. Just a secret I needed to keep. Sports saved me, especially football. Playing the end position meant not having to bulk up plus showing off speed created a spectacular rush. And hearing my friends screaming cheers gave me confidence.

I was untouchable. I was in drama class and because of my football gamesmanship, no one suspected I was gay. Cheerleaders bounced with me. I brought guys into my bedroom after school. I told my mom, "We are rehearsing a scene for our class tomorrow. Please don't disturb us."

Mom and Dad gave me privacy. Because I dated Christian girls and made straight A's, there were no probing questions. The perfect son. When I turned nineteen, I wanted them to know me.

I had finished my first year at Cal State Northridge. I wanted to be a drama teacher. Both parents were proud of me. When we finished our weekly Sunday night dinner I explained, "I love the way you've supported me. Never questioning my decision to get a theater degree. And the hardship of paying for the surgeries to correct my scoliosis. You never push me about dating. I want to tell you I'm gay."

Stunned faces sucked the oxygen out of the room. The clichés shot from their mouths.

"You're going through a phase. What are you talking about? You've dated girls since Junior High. Is this a joke?"

"No, really I'm gay. I don't want to keep secrets from you."

The screaming burst my eardrums. Dad went into my room and began dumping my clothes out of drawers and the closet.

"You're outta here right now. I have no son. Take your stuff and leave."

Mom didn't say a word. When I tried to hug her goodbye, she bristled away from me.

I was banished. I haven't communicated with them in over five years. Now I need to make Matt my boyfriend.

He's such a good sport to follow me to the engine room. Is he really that uncoordinated that he let himself get stuck between the machinery? I'm aroused by the crunching apparatus. He'd blame me if he remained wedged between those engine pipes. The poppers will make him fly. Oh God, he's so yummy. His nervousness is making him delicious. I love men that show their vulnerabilities. But he's right, this area is too small. I don't want to get jammed down here.

"Now be careful as we pass this slim passageway. Don't get trapped. Turn to the side sweetie."

He's being observant as we easily move through the maze. I slip through his fingers and feel his electric current percolate through me. He is loving the magic bench. This is just a sneak preview. I can't wait to get back to the room.

"Oh, my heart is racing. Help me up," he says.

"It's the poppers doing their work. Just go with it." I grab him by the waist and carefully lead him out of the ship's bottom. I love controlling him.

We hold hands as we climb back to my stateroom. As I use my key card and open the door, something seems off. I hear water running. Are we in the wrong cabin? Did I leave the shower running? No way. Matt looks spacey so I lead him to the bed.

"Just get comfy in the bed, Matt."

Matt is stoic. I hope he's not having some sort of adverse reaction to the poppers. Oh no, the water has stopped. Was it my imagination that I heard running water? I've got to piss anyway. I step into the miniature bathroom. Shit, someone is in the stall. I start screaming.

"Wasup?" comes a familiar voice. Oh God, it's Steve.

"What the fuck are you doing here? I thought you cancelled the vacation? My heart feels like it's exploding. Damn."

"Hey, chill, Daniel. I felt so awful about bailing out on you. I spoke to my boss again and he said I could go. I have to sign on every day for an hour in case there's an emergency on the project. It's a bomb. Plus, I got the promotion. I'll be moving at the end of the month."

Ah, with no roommate I'll be unable to remain in the apartment. Matt will be my savior.

"Congrats. Hey when did you check in?"

"Very last minute. Like four-thirty. The traffic was a bitch. But I had this great Uber driver. He wiggled his car around the congestion. I can't believe I made it. You don't look very happy to see me."

"I'm shocked. What have you been doing since you got on board?"

"After I ate, I went to the casino. I got hooked on the slots and tried blackjack. Very cool."

"Look, I met this guy tonight. The room isn't set up for three." I explain to Steve.

"Oh, please. With these twin beds moved together it's like a queen bed. Is the guy quiche?"

"His name is Matt. I want this to work. He has connections at the William Morris agency. He's my inroad. And I enjoy talking to him. He's Jewish marriage material. It's dead."

"Oh wait. You've just met him and already you're planning a serious hookup," Steve replies.

My evening is cancelled. We should have stayed down below. Crap. I don't want to lose this chance. Now we'll have no time to be alone.

"What about a threesome Daniel? Do you think Matt is up for it?" Steve laughs.

"He's out of it now. I had him sniff too many poppers and I don't think it agreed with him."

"He looks old. I don't get you and this thing you have with senior citizens. Come on, let's get him undressed."

Oh God. Is this what I want? A three way with Steve. No, I can't even. It should be special with Matt. But I might not get another chance. Saltiness ripples through my mouth.

Steve starts moving the beds together. When he starts to remove Matt's clothing, I stop him.

"Let me. Hands off." I gently remove each particle of clothing. His dockers, white jockey shorts, and skimpy tee all slide to the floor. I kiss his forehead and whisper in his ear, "I love you, Matt." His chest hairs form a design of a cross. He could be my security blanket.

Steve says, "Okay Mr. Possessive. Let's get to sleep. We're getting off at Cabo tomorrow. I have big plans and you are part of them, Daniel."

I fold into Matt and drift.

Six hours later, the jolting noise wakens my sleep. I dreamed of making sumptuous love to Matt. I am spent. Ah, he's sleeping soundly. His nostrils are tickling my view. The scrambled grey hair flies on the pillow. He's a prize. Such a sweet soul. And he was in my arms all night. Oh, then I remember Steve was in bed too. I can't even process that. Where is Steve? A loud voice shoots through the bathroom.

"We're in Cabo, and we're off for an adventure."

"What about Matt?" I ask. Steve says, "He looks comatose. Why don't we just let him sleep it off while we do our thing in Cabo. And let's check his wallet. These old guys carry lots of cash. We need some extra cash for the weed purchase."

"No way. Wait a minute. Is this some kind of drug purchase?"

"Hey, I've given you plenty of marijuana at a real discounted rate. You owe me."

"I don't owe you anything Steve. I paid you."

I start shaking Matt, "Sleepy head. We're in Mexico. You need to shower and make yourself pretty for the world."

No answer. I'll give him ten minutes while I ready myself. My guardian angel remains in dreamland.

I turn up the hot water so that pellets shoot across my torso. Burning off my old life before I met Matt. I'm reborn today. The boring white towel doesn't do much to absorb my soaked skin. The steam has made the mirror invisible. I open the bathroom door to let the moisture escape. I realize I can't go along with Steve's plan.

"Steve, I am staying. What if he wakes up and starts wondering around the ship?"

"I'll give him something so he'll sleep all day. Don't worry. We'll leave the *Do Not Disturb* sign on the door."

"Forget it. I'm not going with you."

Steve shot back, "Don't expect me to help you with your web page or audition videos. And stop flapping your hands. It's so gay."

Crap, Steve's right. I use my hands when I'm nervous. Not good for an actor. And I'm not tech suave like him. I need those videos for my career.

"We have to get off the ship right now. I'm meeting friends in Cabo and doing a pickup. We can't be late. I need you. We both need to carry back the cannabis in our underwear. There is too much to hide and carry for one of us. Plus, you'll be back up in case something goes wrong."

"No."

"Look, you drugged this guy with poppers last night. You want me to tell the cruise director? You could get into trouble. Plus, you went to the off-limit engine area."

"How did you find that out?"

"Your lover mumbled about it during the night."

"Bullshit. I didn't give him the poppers against his will."

"They're illegal and especially on a cruise with kids. Who knows what else you shoved down his throat? You're in big trouble. How did you even sneak them onto the ship? The X-ray machine didn't catch them?"

"I had them well hidden in my socks deep in my luggage. Impossible to detect. You expect me to be a drug runner with you? That's crazy."

"And what if I told him about your violent temper and how you wrestled in acting class. You lucked out with that. So, don't be a sus. We're just getting supplies for the week. It's great stuff and cheap. Like half the price in the States. It will make this cruise brilliant."

Why did I tell Steve about the wrestling match? I never did go back to that class. That was a year ago. We had an assignment to do a ten-minute wordless scene. I had the bright idea to recreate the wrestling by Alan Bates and

Oliver Reed from *Women in Love*. The D.H. Lawrence novel had been adapted for the screen in 1969. Bates and Reed were wrestling in the nude with a fireplace burning in the background. Larry Kramer did the adaptation so there were subtle gay overtones. This would be a perfect silent performance piece.

I was teamed with Benjamin. He was always baiting me with, "Oh Daniel, why do you have to act so gay? You're never gonna be a star. You need to butch it up. And stop using your arms and hands so much." I tried ignoring him. Ben was a jock on testosterone. Over six feet tall with gobs of blonde hair that he kept flicking with his hand across his forehead. His frown was causing permanent creases in his face. He was jealous of my wiry five-ten sculptured dynamism.

"Look Danny, you can do whatever you want but don't you dare try anything with me. You got that? I'm not gay." He pushed me and walked away.

The acting teacher, Elliot Gringer, forced us to work together. Before we rehearsed at Benjamin's apartment, he told me, "You know I was on the wrestling team at Fairfax High. That's the only reason I'm doing this faggy stuff. Want to add a little realism. Remember just wrestling nothing else, Danny."

I hated being called Danny, sounded like a little kid. I wanted this to work with Benjamin. And we really got into it with the wrestling. Stopping periodically to stare at each other. It was perfect. We were going to kill it when Elliot saw us perform.

We were the first to perform in class. Elliot explained, "This is from *Women in Love*. No dialogue. Let's see what these guys can do with it."

The class was clapping and whistling. They knew we didn't get along and were expecting fireworks.

We faced each other. I circled Benjamin like an animal before the kill. He did the same. We both fell to the floor and tangled. We were in rhythm. Two dancers grabbing, pulling, and choking. Back and forth. Leg scissors and head holds. We growled at each other and stared intensely. Then I rubbed his crotch area by accident. He got up from the floor and began walking away. I went ballistic and threw him down on the ground. I smashed his head against the floor. He reminded me of my father. I yanked his arms until he screamed. I wouldn't stop. Blood began gushing from his nose.

Elliot ran over to us and tried pulling us apart. I couldn't stop until two other students came at me and ripped me off Benjamin.

Ben hollered, "You faggot animal. I'm calling the police. Gonna get you arrested. Fuck."

I heard my heart beating through my chest. I started running. When I left the building, I became nauseous. I stopped to throw up and then continued jogging.

When I got back to my apartment I curled up into the fetal position. I prayed that the police wouldn't burst open the front door and arrest me. I was barely able to sleep through the night. For the next few days, I kept looking behind me, waiting to be handcuffed. Nothing happened. I guess Ben chickened out.

Years later when I told my therapist about this, he said I have infantile anger issues. It's bullshit. Ben was asking for it.

Now, Steve is ruining the cruise. This scheme of his is stupid.

"What if we get caught bringing it back on the ship?" I am trying to talk sense into this jerk.

"The X-ray on the cruise isn't as sophisticated as at the airport. No problem. You stick the weed in your classic tight whitey briefs. Now get your ass in gear. Dress and we are going."

When I gaze at Prince Matt I wonder if he wanted to see Cabo. Well, there are two more stops on the cruise. He'll have his chance to hit the beaches. I nibble on his nutritious lips and say goodbye. And I do love the idea of inexpensive good weed. Matt will be fine.

Friday March 4, 2016 6:00 p.m. Gordon's Cabin

GORDON

Management is incompetent. I'm putting on a detective hat and doing my own investigation. My first agenda item will be to revisit the disco at 11:00 p.m. That's five hours from now. Let's see what's in the daily activity listing to occupy my time. Shabbat Services at 6:30 p.m. Amazing that there are enough people on the ship to make a minion—ten Jews. Deck Nine. I can use some help from God to find Matt. I've got thirty minutes to shave, shower and look presentable to pray.

If Harry were alive, what would he think about me asking for God's help?

Shortly after we met in 1981, we visited his Presbyterian parents in Point Loma, California. Harry was an atheist but in front of his parents he acted religious. I hadn't been in a church since my temporary conversion at sixteen. When the wafer and wine was passed among the congregants, I was partaking in the ritual. That evening Harry told me, "My parents were angry at you. It felt like a slap against their religion that you took the sacraments. It's bad enough that they don't accept our relationship, now they think you are mocking them." Religion strikes again.

We never spoke about God during the next fifteen years. When Harry was diagnosed with AIDS in 1994, spirituality wasn't part of our life.

In January of 1996, Harry's parent made a rare visit. His parents still hadn't acknowledged our relationship. Their standing in the San Diego community surpassed any familial bonds to Harry. The mumbling, "Thank you for taking care of Harry," when they greeted me, felt insincere. Only when death was imminent could they express gratitude. After they left, Harry told me, "They knelt in front of my bed and asked Jesus to save him. I went along with them because I felt they needed this. What would I have gained by being honest with them? That I'm an atheist. I did tell them I had messed up my life."

A week later the destination was Chris Brownlie Hospice. We had decided that my lover Harry would get twenty-four-hour attention that I couldn't provide. I tricked myself into believing I couldn't take a leave of absence from work. My psychologist had asked, "How would you feel if Harry died in your condo?"

"I don't know. I've never seen someone die." When I told my mom that evening, she agreed with the psychologist.

Harry went along with the decision to move to a hospice.

We didn't have a wheelchair. His legs were like twigs so my friends took Harry's emaciated body out of bed and gently placed him on his desk chair. It was like a Jewish wedding where the bride and groom are carried in the air in chairs by the wedding party. Harry grimaced from the maneuver that transferred Harry from the chair to the backseat of my car.

The serenity at the hospice was such a contrast to the zombie-like shuffling of the patients. Gardens of wooded trees crept along the patio of the Hospice.

It didn't take courage for me to say, "I love you" when I left the hospice. Abandoning him shamed me. Selfish, empty thoughts were my relief when I returned home.

Besides my daily visit, only my friend Carl had the strength to see Harry. I was horrified by what Carl revealed, "I had written a poem and read it to Harry. He was going blind. I think he was protecting you. He didn't want you to worry." I didn't realize I needed to be shielded.

Ten days later I received a call at work, "Harry passed early this morning. His heart stopped." I robotically told my boss Harry died, and I left work. When I arrived at the hospice Harry was laying peacefully in his room with cotton pads covering his eyes. I stared at his lifeless form. I couldn't cry. Iced numbness took over. Staring in disbelief. The lyrics of our song "Touch Me in The Morning" took me back fifteen years to our first encounter.

Till you go I need to lie here and think about
The last time that you'll touch me in the morning
Then just close the door Leave me as you found me,
empty like before

I was on auto pilot. I collapsed in my mother's arms later that day. She wouldn't let me crumble but my gutted form was starved for a howl. I yielded to my mother. Mom made the memorial service materialize. She wanted it to be a small gathering, so I excluded his teacher associates, my co-workers and actors from the plays he had written. I worried that my eyes would refuse tears. But when the guys from our AIDS and Shanti support groups showed up, I dissolved into blubber. I wailed into Harry's parents after the ceremony. As I hugged them the rage fury got sublimated. It was the first time they saw the family we created. Yes, they saw our relationship. A little too late. Harry was cremated but his parents had a service in their church in Point Loma. Of course, no mention of AIDS. It was cancer. They never invited me to attend. Further proof about religious twists. Their devout Christianity triggered their homophobia. Instilled a razor thin tie to their son's flesh. The anger burdened me, but I kept in contact with Harry's sisters because it's the only blood tie. I didn't want to erase them from my painful and joyous memories.

My emotional state was fine because I had little inkling about the grieving process.

I had lost my lover of fifteen years. I was thirty-six years old, the same age that my mom was when she became a widow in 1973.

I never reconciled Harry's infidelity. Lacking my father's approval made me think that despite Harry's flaws I had no choice. This is what I deserved. The years of my father badgering me about walking straight from grade school through his death shortly after my Bar Mitzvah, still haunted me at thirty-six. His mantra of "Don't wiggle. Walk Like a Man," fueled my pitiful self-esteem. Despite my relief that I wasn't infected, there was a part of me that struggled to forgive him or myself.

The cliché of being a survivor describes my life after Harry died. Looking back, the complex marriage and philandering were overshadowed by our complimentary personas. We altered each other. His artistic highbrow transformed my pop culture. We kept our passionate highs in tune with Bel Canto Opera and the cabaret torches of Julie Budd. *Valley of the Dolls* could stand with Walt Whitman. Trusting love trumped fidelity norms. The excruciating horrors and deep death-defying love completed me. As I was going through his writings and journals, I found a bittersweet comment about not wanting to live beyond the age forty. He died March 2, 1996 at the age of thirty-nine, four months shy of his birthday. Survival without God. When I started looking for a husband my spirituality changed but now, I need solace from God.

As I enter the small community-type room off the dining room of the ship, I'm startled to see thirty men praying. The bare bones room is nothing like a synagogue. But there is a warmth emanating from the prayer books and flickering candles that illuminate the rectangle space. The vast sea view lets God's presence sneak in. Where are the women? Oh, they are sitting on the side like obedient servants. This must be orthodox. Incomprehensible that orthodox Jews are running services and obeying the misogynistic rituals where women are separated. Our temple is one size fits all. The needs of Orthodox, Conservative and Reform Jews are all satisfied.

Without a leader each congregant is mumbling their prayers with a cantor periodically piping in a chanting song. My spiritual needs aren't going to met tonight. At least they are welcoming me. Handing me a skull cap and prayer leaflet. Matt would be tripping if he was here. Why aren't you here, my dear friend?

The service ends in less than an hour. I'll grab a bite at the buffet. I don't want to sit in the formal dining room and make futile conversation with seven strangers. But I need sustenance to get through this trauma. I can try to get preoccupied by the early show. I'll have to suffer through a magician and comic. I've forgotten about the Friends of Dorothy. They could be aware of Matt and the boy he was dancing with. Excellent, they are meeting at the bar on Deck 9.

Tonight, it's easy to spot the ragtag group of five that are stereotypical GLBT looking, even with the dim lighting. The noise from the gyrating blender, the bartender uses to make drinks, drowns out *I'm Coming Out by* Diana Ross.

"Hi. What a difference from last night. Everyone's out of the closet tonight." A few laughs at my lame humor.

"I'm looking for my friend, Matt. The last time I saw him, he was dancing at the Beehive Dance Club. He never came back to our cabin. Missing in action."

Their sympathetic stares aren't comforting. I want clues or answers as to where Matt is hiding.

"Do you have his picture on your I-phone?" a petite lipstick lesbian asks.

"No, I didn't bring it. I wanted to go social media technology free. Isn't the I-phone useless on the ship?" I explain.

"Describe him for us. I'm Alexa," she asks.

"Matt is five-ten with prematurely grey hair. He's forty-five but looks younger. He has an infectious smile if that helps. His skin is a little discolored from an acne breakout. Was anyone at the disco last night?"

Alexa tells me, "I don't remember your friend but there was a fight. This young kid pushed himself into this large strapping man. He tried to sit on the man's lap. I couldn't tell what started the incident. The boy had long stark black curly hair draped around his face. I could swear he looked like a GQ model."

An African American dressed in shorts and a tank top interrupted, "Hey let me tell the rest. I'm Jackson. The man started shoving and thrust his arms at the boy. The boy wouldn't leave and started screaming, 'I bought you a drink and this is how you treat me.' I swear he was going to belt him. The boy had black eyes that looked like they were shooting darts at the man. Luckily some woman took the man's hand and drew him away from the disco. Must have been his girlfriend. We were so disturbed we left."

The deep voice from this over six-foot guy in a white linen suit jumps in, "No, I stayed around."

Jackson pipes in, "Oh don't listen to Art. He exaggerates. He's such a clothes horse."

Art continues, "But when I checked at midnight, the boy was on the dance floor dragging an older man into this dance marathon. Like two exhibitionists. I could see sweat flying. The older guy was wearing a Hawaiian shirt."

That would be Matt. And the boy he was dancing with had jet black eyes. Wow I've got some important information. We can identify the culprit. I need to get in touch with Henry. It's so late. I'll have to wait until the morning.

My confidence is gurgling.. An uninterrupted sleep will be my reward for my successful sleuthing. In the morning, Henry will be my first stop.

The red blinking light hits my eyes when I return to the stateroom and I wonder why my room isn't made up? As I retrieve the message, I pray that there is news about Matt. It sounds like Henry.

"Gordon, I've been trying to reach you. A couple of things have developed since we spoke earlier. We found a blood-stained Hawaiian shirt on a bench within the engine room. I'm guessing this was Matt's. You can confirm my suspicions tomorrow morning. The second more important item is that someone never made it back to the ship from Cabo. I realize I told you we verified that Matt never left the ship. Apparently, we're missing a guest. Fifteen hundred passengers departed and only fourteen hundred ninety-nine checked back. We're working on finding out who it was. This may resolve Matt's missing status. I just wanted you to know what we found. Come down to my office in the morning."

I'm confused. Why was there blood on the shirt? Oh God. Is Matt hurt? And what does another missing passenger have to do with Matt? Another sleepless night. Too many unanswered questions. The bed invites me to a dreaded depressive version of sleep. My compartmentalizing skills are failing me. I am having withdrawal symptoms from not speaking to Matt for over twenty-four hours as is our ritual

July 2016 Santa Monica

These listless days are wearing away any form of self-esteem. Stuck because Doctor Melnick says no driving. He doesn't want to see friends. Why would they want to be bogged down with a cripple? Doesn't matter if it might be temporary. At least that's what the physical therapist says. And what a pain using Access to get to that appointment rather than a taxi. Yet Access drivers are better equipped to help him on and off his chair. Like an old man using his walker. Where is the van? Lateness isn't an option.

The van arrives before his flaring temper explodes. At the Center for Physical Help, he works with Catherine. She doesn't put up with his bullshit when he screams, "I can't do these exercises." Just don't ask how he's doing.

Thank goodness she starts off with, "Ready for pain?"

****

Friday March 4, 2016 Morning Cabo San Lucas
DANIEL

The brutal heat is melting my skin. I should have over lathered sunblock before we left. I'm going to fry. The humidity is peeling off my face.

If I look past the poverty of Cabo, I become ingrained with Caucasian beaches, infested with tourists. The hand-built jewelry stalls for gringo tourists keep popping into my eyesight. We pass hordes of crowds breaking into the ocean as we walk towards our destination. I'm wearing my bikini speedo in place of underwear. I look so stoked. Steve is wearing jeans, a long sleeve shirt and hat. He doesn't want to change his pasty coloring.

I don't like this plan of Steve's. Steve has been in a foul mood. His cell phone isn't working. He's having trouble figuring out where the location of the drugs will be available for purchase.

"Damn it, Daniel. The GPS is broken. We're fucked. Do you know any Spanish? We need to find the Marina Cordoba area. That's where I was told to meet."

"I'll try to ask." I comply with his request.

"Donde esta, Cordoba?" I mumble to what looks like a locale.

"I speak English. What are you asking?" Thank God.

"We're supposed to meet up with friends in the Cordoba area. Somewhere near the marina," Steve pipes in.

"Yes, take a right at the first major street along this alley. At the end you'll see the Cordoba Marina. Are you sure you want to go? It's unsafe for tourists. Lots of drug traffic."

"That's okay. We have good friends that we're meeting for a few drinks. They know that part of town. Gracias," Steve diplomatically responds. We follow the directions, always looking behind and to our sides, for a surprise. We look like idiot tourists that have gotten lost. A young boy, maybe sixteen, bumps into us. He sticks out his hand and cries out, "Dame dinero." My Spanish is limited but it sounds like he's asking for money.

"No, we don't speak Spanish. No dinero."

He begins frowning. His hand stays in front and he refuses to let us pass. I look at Steve for the next step.

"Just give him some change, Daniel." I search my pocket. I have a few dollars. I shove them in the boy's hand. He begins smiling. He bows as he says, "Gracias." So polite.

"Steve, where are your so-called drug friends? I want to spend some time at the beach."

"Patience. See those fishing boats lined up against the boardwalk. This is the marina area. We need to find a bar. That's where the action is."

Just ahead is a dilapidated store with a tarnished Coca Cola sign above the entrance. A few men are hanging by the door. Is this their version of a bar? Steve motions for me to wait outside while he enters the establishment. I don't quite understand why I'm included in this transaction. Does Steve feel it's safer because he's not alone? Steve believes I'll watch his back. Fuck that.

The brutal sun is pouring on my head. God, it's noon. The worst time of the day to be out. I don't want damaged skin. The face is a major part of an actor's instrument. But wait, I can use this experience when I do my acting exercises. I'll have to thank Steve if I get a part of a drug lord. A breeze is non-existent.

Steve has been gone a long time. Fifteen minutes. Is he getting a drink? This is a dehydration scenario. He said to remain outside. Shit, he could be in trouble. If he's not out in five more minutes I'll butch my way into this dive.

An endless five minutes stagger to a close. I walk into the dark bar. Are they saving electricity? It's such a contrast from the brightness on the street.

"Hello, Steve. It's time to go," I shout.

I don't see him. I lean against the wood bar counter and ask the bartender, "Hi, do you know where my friend Steve is? He came in here about fifteen minutes ago."

He looks at me. Shakes his head and doesn't say anything. He doesn't speak English. I brush past bar stools in search of a back room. The bar is deserted except for a table in the corner. Two older men have beers in front of them. They are laughing as they slurp their Coronas. I would kill for a drink. But I need to find Steve.

At the back of the bar I see a bit of light coming through the bottom of a door. I knock on the door. No answer.

"Hey, Steve are you in there?" I'm scared to barge in. I turn around and begin walking back to the front of the bar. A pointy object starts digging into my back. Oh my God. I'm going to get stabbed. I abruptly turn around and see Steve laughing.

"Fuck you. What's so funny? I thought someone had a knife in my back."

"Just playing with you. I've got the stash in this brown bag. We can go."

"What took so long?"

"Oh, just business stuff. Plus, he gave me a few hits. We are going to get so loaded this week. It will be blessed," Steve chimes back. I grab a coconut drink to hydrate myself before we leave the bar.

The afternoon glides towards the 3:30 p.m.-must-be-back-at-the-ship time. Steve refuses to step into the water. He situates himself in a bar facing the beach while I refresh my bones in the ocean currents. Ripping off my clothes frees any anxiety I felt earlier. Steve watches my wallet, phone and outdoor beach outfit stuffed into the satchel I received as a welcome gift from Carnival Cruise Lines. I gulp the sea breeze and let the water wash over my limbs. I attempt the difficult butterfly stroke. Each exhale of oxygen brutally challenges my lungs. I envision a porpoise or seal or dolphin gravitating through the ocean beside me.

I amuse myself with images of Matt. Being stuck with Steve for the next seven days will be a challenge. I fantasize that Matt will convince his cabin mate friend to give us privacy. I want Matt to myself. No sharing.

I scrape sand off my body and begin toweling off. As I walk towards the bar where I left Steve an alarm goes off. He isn't there. I need my stuff. The boarding I.D. is needed to get back on the ship. He's pissing me off now. An unreliable presence. It's 2:30 p.m., so the window of opportunity to get back to the ship is narrowing. I need nourishment. I would love an ice-tea brimming with ice cubes. I ask the bartender if he can satisfy my thirst. Yes, hibiscus tea. My parched throat explodes with joy as the tea zooms down my throat. He wants to be reimbursed. A familiar voice hits my ears.

"Sorry Daniel. I had to take a dump. Must have eaten something that didn't agree with me. Ready to go back?"

"Yes. I'm spent. I want to see if Matt is okay. Let's go."

"Now remember we're going to hide the stash in your underwear," He reminds me.

"When do we do that?"

"We should go to the restroom here and work that out. Follow me."

"Won't it look suspicious if we're both in the same stall?"

"No, stop worrying. No one cares here. Anyway, the bathroom was empty when I was relieving myself." When we get inside the stall, Steve begins pulling down my speedos as I try to put on fresh jockey underwear.

"Hey, I can do it myself."

"Come on. Can't I play with your basket?"

Oh, now I see where this is going. He wants a quickie before he hides the weed. Damn it.

"No, come on. That wasn't part of the plan. Just tell me how to hide this crap." He pulls the pot out of his brown bag. They are wrapped in plastic.

"Okay just tuck this stuff in your underwear. It will look like you have a large basket when we're done."

"Very funny." I carefully push the cannabis so that my white jockey's stretch. Thank goodness I remembered to switch from my speedos. The jockeys will get out of shape from this exercise.

"Come on. You can fit more in there. Be creative. Here let me help you."

His hands begin shoving more weed against my cock. His sweaty hands keep searching for empty spaces. Oh God. Now he's shoving them in my crack.

"Steve, that's it. I'll look like an idiot when I walk."

"Just put your shorts on and no one will notice. We're done. You're fully loaded. Oh shit. I'm getting a little nauseous. Get out of the stall. I've got to go."

He pushes me through the door and plops himself on the toilet. He starts moaning and I hear the sound of his bowels emptying. And it stinks. Ugh.

I go over to the sink and start washing my hands when I notice a bunch of guys entering. They look at me oddly. They start giggling and pointing to my groin. This was a stupid idea. What are they going to think when I try to board the ship? Fuck. I've got to rearrange the pot so it looks more natural. I go into another stall and maneuver the weed. I check out myself in the bathroom mirror. Well almost perfect. I look hot with a large basket. Like Mark Wahlberg in *Boogie Nights*. The mirror reflects a lobster coloring staring at me. The bronze look is evading me. I'll need to have my skin rehabilitated back at the ship.

"Steve, we need to hustle. The deadline to get back to the cruise is like right now. Get your ass out of there so we can go." No response. He's bolted to the stall.

"Steve," I start shouting. The guys start laughing again. What has happened to Steve? I try jumping to see what is wrong. He is slumped over the toilet. I need help to rescue him.

"Hey guys. Can you help me get my friend out of the toilet? He's sick. Fainted."

They look at me, confounded by what I'm saying. My Spanish skills are nil.

I'll have to crawl under the door. The filth of urine and toilet paper is attaching to my clothes. I try to ignore the stink. My clothes will need to be sanitized or burned when we get back to the Carnival Splendor. Throwing up is not an option during this rescue mission. You are going to owe me, Steve, if I get you out of this catastrophe. I continue sliding through and am able to stand.

I begin shaking him. "Steve, get up." He awakens from his faint and growls at me.

"I'm so sick. I'm afraid to get up from the toilet. I won't make it back to the ship."

"Just suck it up. We have to leave. I'll help you. We're not that far. Come on."

I help lift him from the seat. The vile smell is shooting through my nostrils. Now I'm going to puke.

"Pull up your pants," I tell Steve.

He tries to stand on his own despite his wobbling legs. I open the stall door and lead him out. As we leave the bathroom the heat blasts at us.

"I need some water. I'm afraid I'll pass out again."

"On our way back, we can get some bottled water." I spot a street vendor and grab a bottle of water as I shove him a couple dollars.

Steve starts gurgling the water down his throat like it's a golden potion. He's a zombie brought back to life.

"Oh God. I feel much better. Thank you. Do you remember how to get back to the port?" he asks.

The humungous ship is easily visible as we turn the corner. I can't remember when the last tender leaves. It's 3:45 p.m. I hope it was 4:30 p.m. or we are screwed.

"We need to run or we won't make it."

With the ship in sight, we are able to jog towards our destination. Steve is trying to keep up with me but he's more vulnerable to the heat. The distance between us becomes cavernous. Steve's exhausting breaths are wreaking havoc on his body. He hasn't spent a day in the gym. A workout for him is going from his laptop to the refrigerator. I'll need to sweet-talk the tender crew to patiently wait for Steve.

"I'm going to run ahead and ask them to wait for you if we're late."

"Go ahead. I'm going to be sick again if I continue at this pace."

My speed increases so I can confront the tender staff about the situation. I see a woman sitting under a tent behind a table populated with bottles of water. Our ship sits patiently in the distance waiting for the stragglers.

"Hi, can we wait for my friend? We're late because he was sick."

The woman with a Carnival Crew uniform tells me, "This is the last tender. We're already past the deadline. Where is your friend?"

I look back and don't see Steve. Fuck. We're going to be stranded in Cabo.

"He was behind me. What happens to him if we leave?"

"He'll need to make his own way to our next stop. We can't change the departure time. There is nothing we can do. Do you want to stay and wait for him? Then the two of you can figure out how to get to Mazatlán. You can probably catch a flight."

I need to get back. Matt is waiting for me. Plus, I've got this stuff in my undies. I would never get through an airline X-ray. The ship won't be as stringent.

"Just five more minutes. Please."

June 2016 Santa Monica

The lookout views off of Ocean Avenue gives him a widescreen picture of cloud-laden Malibu to Venice. The last appointment at The Center for Physical Health provided a launching pad of optimism. Catherine, the physical therapist, convinced him there was turtle movement. Perched at the furthest edge of the lookout point, he grips his forearms against the arm rests of the wheelchair. Raising himself to see the ocean makes him feel promise. A deep breath fills his lungs with energy. The throttle from behind kick starts his heart.

"Hey, were you trying to shove me over, old man?"

"You unappreciative prick. Anyway, it's time to head back. I should have gotten you an electric chair. It's tiring pushing you in that thing."

"But you're getting muscles. You're on the way to be called shredded."

"Yeh right."

"Can I take you to lunch?"

"Sure. How are you going to pay for it?"

"Credit card. Come on. Don't be sour. I do appreciate what you've done."

****

Saturday March 5, 2016 morning Gordon's cabin
GORDON

The agitated slumber was interrupted by the need to urinate three times. I obsess about Matt. When we find him, I'm going to reiterate how strongly I love him. Matt has to succumb to this realization. I will stare him down. The friendship will be reframed.

The squealing crunch as we arrive in Mazatlán unsettles my stomach muscles. I'm learning to hate this cruise.

I refuse to shower. I don't care about the crusts imbedded in my eyes. The littered clothes on the floor find their home on my body. I'm going directly to Henry's office. No nourishment.

The banging on his door at 8:00 a.m. wakes my nerves. The door swings open.

"I figured you'd be here this early. Come and sit."

"Just tell me what you've found."

"First I just want to verify that this is Matt's shirt." I pull it to my nose and the whiff of Matt brings tears. The dried blood is frightening.

"Yes, it's his. Where did you find it?"

"The lowest deck of the ship in the engine room. This is an off-limit area. Very dangerous to wander through. I can't imagine why he would be down there. One of the crew was surveying the space and found the shirt."

"That's it? You haven't found anything else? What about the missing passenger?"

"Yes, yes. So, here's the deal. It isn't a passenger that is missing. We think it's a cabin steward. We have an unaccounted crew person. We are concerned that they fell overboard. Guests are complaining that their rooms haven't been serviced.

"So, you're sure that all the passengers that got off in Cabo got back on the ship?" I ask.

"Yes, we're almost 100% sure. I need to be honest with you. There is a slight chance that there was a mix up on the manifest. There are times when there is a rush to get on board right before we depart. I've been told that we had an unusual number of late guests getting back from the tender. We are still verifying the information."

"So, you're telling me nothing new. And here we are in Mazatlán and no answers about Matt. I'm really getting pissed off. There is nothing you can do?"

"We're trying. I've got a team working on it. I ask you to be patient. I know it's been two days. I promise you we'll find him."

****

Friday March 4, 2016 Late afternoon Cruise Ship
DANIEL

We made it. Steve had a splurge of energy to meet the tender deadline. Asking them to wait that extra five minutes prevented Steve from being left in Mexico. My oozing charm worked. Now we are going through the re-check in process. The human scanner looms.

The familiar voice announces, "Please remove everything from your pockets and place your bags and hats on the conveyor belt for X-ray." I drop my hat and small satchel that holds my bathing suit and towel on the tray. Please God don't let them do a body search. I don't want to recreate a scene from *Midnight Express* where Brad Davis gets arrested for drug possession. I walk assuredly with my calm face through the X-ray metal detector doorway to hell. My pores sigh in relief as I realize no bells or whistle alarm hit my ears. I stride towards my room.

"Ah, sir. Please come back."

No, they've found something. I turn in dread.

"You forgot your bag."

He hands me the meager possessions. How can I not smirk? I wait for Steve to follow.

Anxiety over getting to the cabin and seeing Matt overpowers me. An adrenalin rush pushes against my chest.

Upon reaching our cabin I see the *Do Not Disturb* sign is still up. No made up bed or fresh towels will greet us. Matt's image is exposed as we survey the room. My angel is sleeping.

I lean down and kiss his lips. I am startled by the puffy chapped sandpaper quality. They grind into my mouth.

"Hey sleepy head. Wake up. What have you been up to all day?" No response. I begin shaking his head.

"Hey Matt. Stop, fooling around with this groggy act."

He pushes me away and croaks, "Let me sleep."

"You need to drink something. You've been in bed all day. Steve get me some water from the bathroom sink."

Steve obeys and brings a plastic cup brimming with tap water. I gently try to get Matt to drink.

"Just take a few sips."

He cries out, "No."

"Come on baby. You need this." His eyes look glassy. Even with matted grey hair and creases in his face from his elongated sleep, he is swoony handsome. He slurps the water.

"Good. Good. You should feel better soon."

Steve says, "Leave him alone. He wants to sleep it off."

"Steve, what did you give Matt? He's acting strange. Do we need to take him to the ship hospital?"

"I gave him something harmless. I take it all the time. I wanted him out of it to make sure you came with me to Cabo."

"But he had alcohol and poppers earlier."

"You worry too much. He's going to be fine. I don't think it's a good idea to take him to the infirmary. Won't it look suspicious? Are you going to tell them about the drugs we gave him?"

"He could die if we don't get him help."

"Hey, you need to remove the pot from your jockeys. You're going to ruin them if you've been sweating down there."

"I don't get jock itch. Let me rip these clothes off and shower."

I begin peeling the marijuana packets that have stuck to my skin. Steve's hands grab and tickle me. I giggle just to give him a thrill. He'll realize that his form of foreplay isn't going to work. He places each prize into the money safe. You'd think they were diamond jewels.

Now that the marijuana has been dismembered from my genital area, Steve says, "I'm starving. The buffet is calling me. Should I wait for you until after you shower? I'm beyond empty from all my bathroom excursions today." Only Steve would go to dinner in his stinky sweat-driven clothes without cleaning up.

"No, I'm taking a lush, shower. I want to spend alone time with Matt."

"Whatever you want. You're not going to get any action out of him."

This shower is going to be a quickie. Matt needs my attention while the irritation has left.

I scrub underarms, ass and cock. I'll use the boat's shampoo to remove the grime from my hair.

The room is so warm that a once-over with a towel is sufficient. The wet follicles feel hot and sexy.

Snuggling into Matt makes me airborne. Easy to love. I'm insulating Matt and bringing him back to life. As I try to kiss this man, I get no reciprocation. The lips aren't moving. Lifeless. The effects of the shots and poppers must have subsided by now. Could the mysterious drug Steve gave him this morning cause this incapacitation? Is something seriously wrong with Matt? Should I take him to the infirmary? Now my stomach is sending hunger signals to my brain. I haven't eaten much today. I'll go to the buffet. I can ask Steve what he thinks we should do. I kiss Matt goodbye and leave the room.

As I enter the hallway a pounding sensation bludgeons my forehead. I fall against the wall to regain balance. I hug the wall and return to the room. I'm going to be sick. The retching comes fast and furious. My stomach has been devoured. I crawl back to bed. I can commiserate with Matt.

****

Friday March 4, 2016 Evening Buffet Line
STEVE

Oh God. All this free food. I don't think I can fit another item on my plate. Fried chicken, three-bean salad, deviled eggs, fried rice, roast beef, sushi, and biscuits with gravy. I will never leave the ship. And with the stockpiled weed in the room, these seven days will be a gargantuan mindfuck. I don't trust Daniel. He's going to sabotage the vacation. He's so lame. His ridiculous dreams of being a famous star. It's not going to happen. Yeh, he's got that cuteness going for him. I've seen him rehearse scenes and I couldn't help from gagging. No talent. Why does Daniel want to get involved with Matt? He seems like a weird creep.

And this bullshit about taking him to the infirmary. Such a drama queen. Where is he? He was supposed to meet me at the buffet. I hate eating alone. I feel like people are staring at me. I can't even find a table. And this tray is heavy with miles of food on it. I'm forced to ask, "Is it okay if I sit here?"

"It's fine. I'm almost done." The elderly man answers as he looks up from his John Grisham novel. I can't remember the last time I read a book. I get all the information I need from Google.

I don't want to chat. Just shoveling food into me is enough.

"Is this your first cruise?" he asks.

"Yes. Cabo was astonishing."

"I stayed on the ship. Did you hear about the missing passenger?"

I guess I'll be conversing.

"No. What's going on?" I ask.

"There was an announcement last night. I don't remember the full description. Something about grey hair and a Hawaiian shirt. You hear about passengers falling off a ship. That would be horrible."

I hope this isn't about Matt. And what's the deal about him missing? What hasn't Daniel told me? Why would a search to find Matt be occurring? I need to get back to our cabin.

I quickly finish the food. This combination isn't sitting well with me. I don't want to puke.

The *Do Not Disturb* sign is still on the door. As I enter the room the two lovebirds are wrapped up like a sandwich. I've never understood this cuddling. And I don't get sex. But I would like to do it once with Daniel. I could brag about it online.

All I've ever done is jack off to porn. Why bother hassling with dating? And these days the porn sites are so sophisticated. Tumblr is the best. I don't need to go out. It doesn't matter what I'm wearing. It's a waste of time to shower and shave. Stress free. No worries about performing.

This is boring watching them sleep. Oh wait. I have weed. That will take the edge off. I anticipate the high that will smother my tedium. Now, I'll go back to the buffet. I never got a chance to try the desserts.

Matt and Daniel ignore me as I leave with, "So long guys." They both seem very quiet. I see some drool in the corner of Matt's mouth. And there is a smell of urine. Was there an accident?

I start shaking Daniel. "Hey, you need to get up. I think Matt wet the bed."

Daniel is slow to respond, "What's happening? What time is it?"

"You've been sleeping for the last hour while I was eating upstairs. You okay?"

Daniel rambles, "No, I felt faint and nauseous. I never made it past the hall. I collapsed into bed. Too much sun and I must have picked up a bug in Cabo."

"You did get color. And Matt looks pale. Maybe you were right. He should be taken to the ship's infirmary You know, I think Matt is considered a missing person."

"What are you talking about?"

"This guy I was sitting at in the buffet dining room said there was an announcement about a missing person."

"What should we do? Are we in trouble?"

"Ask him."

"Hey honey. Wake up. I think you made a mess in the bed. We need to clean up."

"Let me sleep," Matt mumbles.

"Looks like he's been drugged and kidnapped. You're in a shit-load of trouble. I wouldn't notify anyone about his whereabouts until he's sober."

"Matt, come on. I'll help you shower. The steward needs to come by and clean the bed. Steve, see if you can find someone."

I check the hallway and notice a man standing behind a cart piled with towels, shampoo, and tissues. He smiles at me.

I ask, "Can you change the bedding in our room-5631?"

"Are you going to eat? I can do it while you are out," he asks. I go back to our cubicle.

"He wants us to leave the room so he can change the linen. Are you both well enough to get some dinner?"

"Yes. Give us thirty minutes to shower and dress," Daniel replies.

Matt looks worse. I'm no babysitter.

"I'm going back to the dessert buffet. You seem to have things under control."

July 2016 Santa Monica

The gel from the ultrasound captures the nerves in his legs. Catherine asks, "Are you doing your exercises?"

"Yes, almost every day. I still can't sleep," he responds.

"Restless leg syndrome maybe?"

She begins kneading her knuckles up and down his spinal-cord.

"Just stir crazy. My days are endless and boring. Ow, that hurts."

"Good. I'm breaking down the scar tissue. The muscles need to be invigorated. Are you able to get out of the wheelchair?"

"When I go to the bathroom, I'm able to lift myself onto the toilet seat. I can stand for a short time to shave. But I need to lean against the sink for support."

"Excellent. Emotionally, how are things? That is part of the healing process."

"Complicated. I miss working. And the living situation is complex."

****

Friday March 4,2016 Evening Daniel's Cabin

DANIEL

I can't even get Matt out of bed. Maybe the steward can help us. I think his name is Alfonso. Now that Steve has left, I can focus my attention on getting Matt invigorated. I step out of the cabin and look for Alfonso. He isn't around. Another steward comes into my view.

"Hey, can you ask Alfonso to come to our stateroom? I need to get my friend out of bed and showered so you can change the sheets."

"I haven't seen Alfonso for a few days. I'm Jose. I've been assigned to his cabins."

He quickly comes into the room and helps me pull Matt out of bed. He feels like a wobbly doll as we march him into the shower. I'm praying that once the water hits Matt, he'll recover.

The steward looks concerned, "Your friend looks very sick. Should I get a doctor?"

"No, he just has a hangover. Once he showers, he'll be fine. Thank you."

I go to the bathroom to check on Matt while Jose does his sheet magic. Matt is sitting on the bathroom floor asleep. My nausea returns and I squeeze over Matt to sit on the toilet bowl to relieve toxins. At the five-minute mark, I hear the door slam. Jose must be finished.

I wake Matt and I'm able lead him into the shower like a ragdoll.

The steam-infused shower brings him back to life. I'm socketed to this man. The embrace roars through my testicles. The splashing water doesn't hinder my kissing each orifice of Matt. He moans as the shackles of alcohol and poppers are exhumed from his body. The hairs of Matt's chest comingle with my fuzz. The steam fills up my nostrils.

I can hardly hear Matt when he says, "Let me love you." Passive to aggressor.

Matt continues with, "I need my inha…." He starts wheezing.

After he's facing me, I turn to shut the water off. A flickering moment holds my breath. He collapses into me. As I crumble to the ground, my back grinds against the shower floor. His weight digs into me. A sparking pain throbs around my skin. He's clutched me into a paralyzed state. Unable to move, I scream. The scalding water continues plummeting against both of us. I try to push Matt away but I'm trapped. My legs aren't working. Has he crushed my spine? Matt is non-responsive. And there is blood dripping from his head. The waves of water are clogging the drain. He must have hit his head when he fell on me. The traveling pain engulfs my brain. I'm gone.

Friday March 4, 2016 10 p.m. Ship casino.

STEVE

I'm ahead $200. Pretty good for the slot machines and the blackjack table. Mesmerizing fun. It's almost as hypnotic as when I'm gaming. But this guy with a cigarette keeps staring at me. This tobacco-infested casino is nauseating. Nothing like the sweet weed smell. But this man's parched face has a goofy trickster look. A twig-thin six feet. He must be into fashion with his pink shirt and leopard shoes. I could go for someone like that. I'm hopeless with one-liners. Sweet. He's coming towards me. I don't know where to look. Too scary to look at him.

"Doing well tonight?" he asks.

"Yes. First time charm. What about you?"

"I'm not much of a gambler but I wanted to check out the place. I'm bored. Plus, this is one of the few places I can smoke on the ship."

"Got it. I'm Steven."

"Patrick. Are you alone?"

"Well, sort of. I'm sharing a cabin with my roommate from Los Angeles."

"Oh. Just roommates?"

"Yes. He says I'm not his type."

"Fool. You're cute."

No one ever compliments my fat ass.

"Can I buy you a drink?" Patrick asks.

"Perrier."

A beat passes and he brings me a glass. We click glasses together and smile.

"Thank you, Patrick. I had grass earlier so I'll skip any liquor."

Patrick says, "I get it. We all have our vices. Vodka tonic jazzes me."

"Did you enjoy Cabo?"

"Oh yes. The beach was a milestone of happiness. The locals tripped me up. Joy from the moment I left the ship. Hey, this casino has done it for me. Want to come back to my room?" Patrick asks.

"Yeah, why not. Do you have a roommate?"

Patrick laughs, "No way. I got a great single supplement deal. The space is mine. Come on."

I love his pushiness. Dragging me to his room. I need pics or this didn't happen.

When we enter his cabin, he throws me on the bed. This wiry man muscles his way into me. Pulling off my clothes feels like a scary invasion of my space. I'm embarrassed to admit to Patrick this is my first time. Confusion hides. My shriveling hits my brain.

"Are you nervous? Too fast for you. What do you like to do?"

I pull out my poppers and spring back from my shrunken state.

"Oh, baby is here for me," he purrs.I start crying when my orgasm comes. The sensory touch is altering me. The shaming of my image has crippled me. Being fat and ugly were excuses to hate myself. I don't understand why Patrick is seeing past that. I welcome sleep and the sweetness of sharing the bed with another man for an entire night. But after an hour of being locked into Patrick, my limbs cramp. The electric current permeating through my sleeping arm wakes me. I push Patrick away to recapture free space. His slumber continues unaffected by my movement. I stare at the ceiling. The fire sprinklers smile. The stale air seeps into my nostrils. How do I evacuate back to sleep? Picking new passwords lulls me back to bliss. When I get back on line, I'll use them break the internet.

****

Saturday March 5, 2016 4 a.m. Cabin Shower
DANIEL

I must have blacked out. Matt is still comatose. I need to free myself. And the shower is continuing to spurt water. Flooding the floor. Fingers are wrinkling as the water engulfs the shower. Where is Steve? If he'd come back to the room, he could get Matt off of me. This dead weight is assaulting me. Why can't I slide away? My acting visualization techniques are failing. And how would Lee Strasberg teach me to escape? Houdini would be a better professor. My sleeping legs are immovable and the throbbing spasms running up and down my back are gnawing away my energy. The familiar pain when they corrected my curvature of the spine in high school. Shaking Matt has been a disaster. The pain signals hitting my brain are intolerable. I'm going to try using my arms to extract my torso from Matt. At least screaming gives me emotional relief. Doesn't anyone hear my wailing? I can hear when passengers walk by our cabin. The realization that it's the middle of the night dips my hopes.

I hear a creaking sound.

"Help, Help, Help" I cry out. My screams hoarse my vocal cords. Please let someone hear me.

****

Saturday March 5, 2016 8:30 a.m. Patrick's cabin
STEVE

The sun creeps through the window. I need to untangle Patrick's grip. I hate the way he is clinging to me. So needy. And I want to go back to my cabin. Too long since I ingested weed. I need more Vicodin. Patrick is oblivious to my nervousness.

"Patrick, I'm going back to my room," I tell him. He throws a pillow on his head and returns to his slumber.

I grab my pants and shirt. After I piss, I glance at the mirror. The folds of my stomach don't insult me. My face pallor is colored from Cabo's sun. This no-longer-a-virgin persona is pleasing. But I still want my weed.

The walking pace quickens through the hall. Disparaged food sits in the front of cabin doors. The luxury of ship room service. The smell of leftovers is stomach-turning.

As I enter our cabin, I encounter a squishy sound emanating from my shoes. The soggy, water-logged carpeting is out of place. No sign of Matt or Daniel. There are blood stains in the bathroom. I go directly to the safe to ensure my stash is in place. Thank goodness nothing has been moved. This mysterious flood and missing cabin mates are disconcerting. I wouldn't be surprised if Daniel took Matt to the infirmary. And what could Matt possible tell them that wouldn't incriminate me or Daniel himself? Now that I have my stash I can go back to Patrick's and hangout until this furor dies down. I don't have any options. They know I'm Daniel's roommate. I'm going to lay low until I find out what Matt has said.

As I leave the room, I'm accosted by two uniformed men.

"Are you Steven Merriman?"

"Yes. What's wrong?"

"Your cabin mate is in a hospital in Mazatlán. We need to question you about what happened last night. Please come with us."

Saturday March 5, 2016 4:30 a.m. Daniel's cabin

DANIEL

The door opens. Rescuers have arrived. Two men grab hold of Matt pulling him off me. Matt starts coughing. Thank God Matt is okay. I begin shaking as they shut off the shower. The freedom from the dead weight brings me to tears. Agony erupts as men grip my shoulders. "Can you get up?"

"No, I can't move my legs" I tell them. Shivering in my nakedness, I implode. Pain comes rushing back and I resume blankness.

****

Saturday March 5, 2016   8:30 a.m. Henry's Office
GORDON

My defeated departure from Henry's office is interrupted by a shout.

"Gordon, come back. We think we've found your friend." Henry tells me.

"Where is he? Oh God, is Matt okay?" I start hyperventilating.

"Two guests were brought to the infirmary early this morning. One of them may be Matt. I was told they were unresponsive so identification can't be confirmed. All I know is that there were two injured men. One suffered a concussion. The other guy is being sedated because of severe pain. Let's go to the infirmary."

I try absorbing the information without passing out. The electrodes traveling through my middle back explode.

I can only walk at a gingerly pace. The balls of my feet are fired up but I'm able to follow Henry. As we enter the infirmary a silence permeates the room. Henry begins talking to the nurse.

"We're here to see the injured passengers."

The nurse explains, "We had to transport them to the Mazatlán Hospital."

Henry responds, "But I was just told they were discovered."

"The head doctor made the decision that it was best that they be moved. The injuries were quite serious. One of them was wheezing from an asthma attack and could hardly breathe. You'll need to talk to Dr. Martinez."

The nightmare continues.

"Henry, I want to go to the hospital. If Matt is there, I need to see him.

"Let me facilitate that."

****

Saturday March 5, 2016 9:30 a.m. Mazatlán Hospital
GORDON

The taxi speeds through the streets of Mazatlán until we reach our destination. The throngs of locals and tourists unsettles my stomach. My petrification of Matt being in a foreign hospital and the care he'll receives tops my list of worries. And this putrid heat is nauseating. When we arrive, Henry asks at the front desk, "We're looking for two injured guests from the Carnival ship. They would have been brought to the hospital this morning. Do you have any information? Can we see them?"

Their response in Spanish raises my fret. Henry responds in the Spanish dialect. He turns to me.

"They are doing lab work, X-rays and a whole host of tests. We'll need to wait."

"Is it Matt?"

"I don't know. Since it was an emergency, they were both admitted without any identification. They know they are from the vessel and had passports or they wouldn't be able to sail. We need to be patient."

At the three-hour mark, I am led to a hospital room.

The dimly lit space doesn't give me any confidence that Matt is in good hands. The overpowering machines hooked up to him raises my level of apprehension. As I approach the bed, I am aghast. It's not Matt. Who is this? The other passenger. I immediately turn around and march into the hallway. I need a nurse to point me to another room.

"I'm looking for the other patient from the Carnival cruise," I plead with the standby nurse. She points me down the hall to another space.

As I enter the room, there are machines hooked up to the patient. A white sheet covers most of his body. I can't tell if he's sleeping. I can't recognize who it is because of his bandaged head. My anxious tears spurt as I walk towards him. His neck is held in some sort of vice. The heavy breathing comforts me despite the damaged head. As I lean towards him, my back spasms. I keep ignoring the deterioration of my vertebrae. I grip hold of the bed to steady myself as I whisper.

"Matt, It's Gordon." The anxious waiting creates a butterfly effect on my heart. Matt's unresponsiveness makes me gently shake him. The fluttering eyes spring into action. A smile changes the contours of his face.

"Hi. I really screwed up, didn't I?" he croaks. Like Sleeping Beauty awakening from years of slumber with a deep bass voice.

"Thank goodness you were found. You really banged your head."

"I've got a doozy of a headache. I messed up my neck. Bruised the nerves. I can hardly move my legs. The doctor said it might a few weeks before the swelling goes down. Then they'll know if I have any permanent damage. I feel leg cramps and pain so I guess that's a good thing. And on top of that I had an asthma attack. I didn't have my inhaler with me. Where's Daniel?"

"Who's Daniel?"

As I listen to his Daniel story my anger is reduced because my friend has been returned to me.

"Did he drug you?"

"No, I knew what I was doing. Combining poppers and alcohol was a stupid choice. Although I vaguely remember swallowing some other pills."

"This Daniel is a jerk. You could have died."

A doctor comes by and tells us the next twenty-four hours are critical. Matt needs to be watched. At that point we can fly back home. But the other man is in worse shape. He may be paralyzed. The blessing of an English-speaking physician swells through me. His Doctor George Clooney-handsome appearance is a refreshment.

Matt's uncontrollable sobs break me. This Daniel must have taken hold of Matt. Is Daniel responsible for Matt's injury?

"Do you remember what happened"

"No, I just remember waking up in the shower and attendants pulling me off Daniel. He sounded like a wounded animal as I broke free. I'm worried that I fell on him in the shower. I let my cock rule me."

"I accidentally visited his room before I came to see you."

"There was a linking bond with Daniel. It felt like a religious experience. You know how you would tell me how you felt after a first date. I never understood how an initial contact could create a combustible spark. I knew the relationship would flame out based on your history. The passion was something I had never experienced. When I met Daniel, an unknown aching thirst was quenched. I let the barrier filters down. Can you tell him I'm sorry?"

I say, "Yes," without really meaning it.

"I hate losing control. It's not me. Is it, Gordon?"

A momentous kiss pops.

"I love you Matt. I'm sorry I never told you. Is there room for us to love each other?"

His eyes droop to sleep. I don't need to look any further than his soulful eyes before they withered. An honest answer from Matt scares me.

As I leave the room, I inch towards the area where Daniel resides. I'm curious as to what was so special about this boy that connected with Matt. I knock on the door and hear a barely audible, "Come in."

"Hi, I'm good friends with Matt. I wanted to introduce myself."

The uncomfortable pain in his eyes are pronounced. The demon black eyes create fear.

"Can you adjust the sheet for me?"

I look at Daniel. The innocence of his youth beams towards me. I move the sheets so his feet are covered.

"Matt wanted to say he was sorry he hurt you."

"Oh no. It's my fault. I should have never given him poppers. I'm an idiot."

"Matt can be a charmer. He knew what he was doing with the drugs."

With a tear inching out of Daniel's eyes, I want to smother his agony but I can't rise to this honor. The ache in my back and feet throb. The rage at Matt for subjecting me to the last forty-eight hours won't subside. Who would have thought that trying to overcome my fear of the ocean would be trumped by this nightmare?

I leave Daniel's room and head back to Matt. Flashing lights rattle the building. Nurses and doctors are speeding by my shoulders. My angered feet quicken their pace but I stop cold when I realize they are entering Matt's room. I'm pushed aside as they slam the door. I collapse to the floor in a tear-stained anxiety fit. I just saw Matt and he was fine. Upon standing I attempt to look through the window as to what action is being taken. The array of humans hovering over Matt frightens me. My shallow breathing makes me lightheaded.

The dead silence permeates. The door opens as each defeated doctor and nurse escapes. I rush in only to find Matt's sheet covering his face. Impossible. I need clarity. I grab hold of a doctor and stare him down until he talks.

"I am so sorry. We tried. We think his lungs were damaged from his asthma attack. And when Matt hit his head, it caused an undetected brain aneurism. I told you the first twenty-four hours were critical. We thought the X-ray could give us a clue."

I fold to the ground. Agony permeates. The doctor attempts to help me up without success. The fragile bones along my vertebra are rebelling. The tendonitis in the feet send up flares.

"I need a wheelchair. I have multiple herniated discs that are inflamed. My feet are a mess also."

As a nurse swings down the hall, he asks her to get a wheelchair. Within minutes, I collapse into the chair, I regain some semblance of normalcy.

The tasks racing through my brain are competing for priority. Contacting Matt's relatives. Getting back to Santa Monica. Coping with my own disability. Anything to avoid grieving.

"Can you contact Henry? He's the ship officer that brought me here. I need help."

****

Saturday March 5, 2016 10:30 a.m. Mazatlán Hospital

DANIEL

My panic mode is fired up. The shock of meeting Matt's roommate, Gordon, distracted me from the clusterfuck situation I'm in. My legs aren't working. I'm stuck in a foreign country. I can't think about who I can contact to extricate me from this jam. Parents are off limits. That jerk Steve is useless. And I have no money resources to pay for this emergency. But Matt's condition is preying on me. At least he has Gordon to look after him. This assault on my body is exhausting.

Just as I try to doze off the siren flashing sounds whip around the outside of my room. What is going on?

May 2016 Santa Monica

GORDON

I never thought I could accomplish ten thousand steps a day. The miraculous back and feet recovery is in full swing. Weeks of being confined to a wheelchair was humiliating. Not one to ask for help, I wallowed in being disabled in my condo. I allowed the barest of assistance. Driving to doctor appointments. Ordering food from local haunts served me well. The mourning waves of Matt wash at the most inopportune times. At the Montana Street Pavilion, a windfall hit me at the seafood counter. The Santa Monica Seafood salmon was the sure-fire entrée I served when we ate together. The last three months are full of incorrigible events.

Henry facilitated my flight home. I never did learn what happened to Daniel. Henry said something about Daniel's roommate. There was suspicion of an overdose of a dangerous drug being responsible for Matt's death. But Matt's sisters didn't want to level any charges after I told them what I suspect had happened. We all wanted to wipe the Mexican Cruise from our memories.

Matt's sisters had arranged the funeral with my non-functioning disabled body unable to organize the event. The rabbi used her soothing powers to unblock grief. I welcomed the hordes of congregants that supplied me with food and solace. The clockwork tasks eliminated any emotional baggage I was carrying. Netflix became a treasured friend. Binging on *House of Cards* hid my multitude of angry episodes. These vacancies from the death of Harry, my mom and now Matt are taking their toll.

My therapist says I need a project. Doesn't he believe in the six stages of grieving?

When my cell phone rang an unfamiliar number appeared. Should I let it go to voice mail in the event it's a robocall? I'm emotionally replenished today. I'll wing answering it.

"Hello. Who is this?"

"Daniel."

The wrench tightens around my gut.

"I'm sorry I couldn't reach you to give my condolences when Matt died. I was just released from the hospital."

I don't want to hear this voice. How did he even get my number?

"My ex-roommate, Steve was a computer geek. He was able to find your cell number."

"What do you want?"

"I know you're angry. While I've been in the hospital, I've had nothing to do but think about Matt. The thing is I don't have any place to live. Steve moved out of town. And I'm in a rehab facility just till the end of this week. Medi-Cal won't pay for anything beyond this Friday. You'll probably think I'm crazy, but I was wondering if I could."

"I can't talk." I press the red hang up button on the phone.

My ears hear a silent scream. And my day was going so well.

The lounge chair becomes a cocoon. Raging anger rivets gushing tears. The pitting hole Matt gave me is scraping the fibers of the chair. The heightened touch sensation frightens me.

May 2016- Santa Monica

GORDON

For the last week I've had a recurring nightmare about Matt and Daniel. The image of them in the shower complicated with their time spent in the Mazatlán hospital gives me night sweats. The soaked sheets remind me of Harry. The way AIDS had ravished his immune system. The wet sheets that had to be washed daily.

The guilt is overpowering me since I hung up on Daniel. I rehash the cataclysmic cruise that I coerced Matt into going on. I wouldn't let Daniel speak. Is there a brave cell in my bones to call him back? I'm terrified I'll say something monstrous to him.

If I took drugs or drank, the courage I'd need would rise. Fuck it.

I glance at my iPhone and redial Daniel's number. I don't believe in signs but it's a link to Matt.

"It's Gordon. Sorry I hung up on you."

The long pause ends with Daniel talking, "I figured you'd be bitter. Look I hate talking on the phone. And what I'm proposing should be done in person. Is there any way you could come to the rehab hospital? A face to face?"

God, what an infringement.

"I guess so. Where is it?"

On my arrival, my shattered nerves skip off the pavement with each step. The West Los Angeles raggedy convalescent home doesn't bode well. I ask for Daniel Erickson and am told to go to the end of the naked hallway. I would kill myself if I had to stay in this location. The antiseptic doom screeches from the neutral walls. The shock wave of seeing an unshaven Daniel in a wheelchair wearing a hospital gown makes me gulp. The black hair is shorn to a crew cut. The sound of the television echoes. The credits for the daytime Soap Opera *Young and The Restless* flares across the screen.

"Hi Daniel."

"Oh my god. I didn't realize you'd be here so soon. Thank you for coming. Let me mute the television."

"I can only stay for a short time. I have an appointment." I lie not wanting to drag this awkwardness any longer.

"I need a temporary place to stay. I know this is insane to ask you."

"Wait a minute. You want to move into my condo? I would never." But as I say the words, memories of Matt flash.

"I understand. I don't have any options unless I contact my parents. They don't want to hear from me." His empty black filled eyes take me away from my thoughts. Confusion whips me silent.

"I knew it was a long shot. You can go. I have physical therapy. They tell me there is a chance I can regain movement in my legs. That I'd be able to walk again. A rare chance the nerves will regenerate from the compression. Even if I'm left with a limp." He stops mid-sentence.

I hear an explosive bang and realize that Daniel has thrown the T.V. remote against the wall. The device lays splattered on the floor. His outburst turns to sobs. Anxiety confronts my decision to flee. But I summon Matt's presence. His aura whispers, "Gordon, please."

I turn back and enter his wheelchair space.

"I'm crazy to propose this. Yes, I'll take you in. Temporary arrangement. Just till you can walk. Matt would have wanted me to do this."

Daniel's cries remain in full force. I am forced to comfort him. I have a love/hate relationship with my caretaking role. I bend to his level and grasp both his hands. The emotional guard rails burst apart and I empty my own tears. Mourning takes its toll. And as Daniel's eyes absorb their tears a trace of a smile forms. I let myself grin.

"Look what you've done to us, Matt. Sniveling babies grieving."

Bio

After spending forty years as an accountant, Gordon retired in 2017 and started a new career as a writer. During 2020, Gordon had published work in Wingless Dreamer, Two Hawks Quarterly, The Doctor T.J. Eckleburg Review, Gay Wicked Ways and Emeritus Chronicles. He's a standup comic who has performed at Canters and The Blackbox Theater at the LGBT Village in Hollywood. His stories recorded at AKBAR in Hollywood are available on the Queer Slam podcast called "Just Gordon."

https://podcasts.apple.com/.../episode-21-just-/id1446511726...

When he isn't writing he'll be cooking gourmet gluten-free meals, reading the latest Elin Hilderbrand novel, watching Alfred Hitchcock films, listening to anything by Barbra Streisand, walking 7,500 steps a day, or getting writing inspiration from his friends Sy and Charlie. Gordon has been a member of the oldest GLBT temple in the world, Beth Chayim Chadishim since 1990 and has given multiple sermons.

www.ingramcontent.com/pod-product-compliance
Lightning Source LLC
Chambersburg PA
CBHW061400250726
48657CB00004B/1593